UPGRADE YOUR HOUSE

Contents

Introduction

So you own a home that's not exactly in mint condition, and you want to fix it up, either because you're getting ready to sell it, or you just want to increase the value and make it a bit more livable. You're willing to tackle some projects on your own, but you're not sure where to start, and maybe you can't decide which projects are really worth doing. One thing you know for sure is that money and time are tight. This book is for you.

The projects we've compiled here are all quick home upgrades that represent the biggest bang for your buck. Forget about $10,000 kitchen remodels, fancy decorative makeovers, or grand room additions—those are for folks with different goals and bigger pocketbooks. What you want are easy (yet legitimate) repairs and inexpensive (yet attractive) upgrades that require only a modest investment of time and money, and little or no professional help. That's why this book is all about the changes you can do yourself that will cost very little besides your labor, and will add the maximum amount of value to your home.

We've included improvements to just about every room in the house so that you can pick and choose the ones that make the most sense for your home and your situation. Keep in mind that kitchen and bathroom renovations are going to have the biggest impact on resale value. But then again, your goal might just be a more comfortable and inviting living room. No matter which project you choose, it's not going to take a big chunk out of your busy schedule; no project in the book will take more than a weekend, and most can be done in just a few hours.

And you certainly don't need to be an expert craftsman to complete the projects outlined here. All the do-it-yourself tasks described in these pages require only basic skills and a modest set of tools. If you can handle a screwdriver, hammer, level, and paintbrush, you've pretty much got all the skill you'll need to tackle any project included here and do a job you'll be proud of at the end of the day.

To make the work even easier, we've supplied a wealth of useful, moneysaving tips and insights. These contain specialized techniques used by contractors, tradespeople, and realtors to boost home value, save a few bucks, or just make the job at hand a little easier. The tips are designed to complement the projects and help you in selecting the right materials, finding shortcuts, and making the right choices throughout the process.

If you're prepping a house for sale, scan the book for obvious upgrades, such a shiny new sink, that will help make strong, positive, and lasting first impressions on any potential buyer who walks in. On the other hand, if you're going to be living in your home for the foreseeable future, focus on projects that add value while also creating a more comfortable and pleasing living space. Either way, grab your tools, flip the page, and get to work on polishing your diamond in the rough so that it shines for family, friends, and potential buyers alike.

Updating the Kitchen

As the heart and hub of the modern home, the kitchen is the single-most important room for improvements. Friends, family, and prospective buyers all gravitate toward this social center, and the kitchen often sets the tone for the rest of the house. That's why it's essential that it be clean, inviting, and aesthetically current.

Whether they're selling or simply renovating, people tend to go a little nuts in remodeling a kitchen. It's understandable. Watch a couple of well-crafted commercials or walk around the glitzy room scenes set up in the local home center, and it's easy to get wrapped up in the idea of new solid-granite countertops and commercial-grade appliances. It's really not difficult to quickly spend thousands of dollars, and even tens of thousands of dollars, redoing a kitchen. But it's also not necessary.

That's because the most appealing kitchen is one that is—first and foremost—tidy, comfortable, and well thought out. When a kitchen is in order and the design serves the function, meals are a pleasure to prepare and the space is an irresistible magnet for eating and socializing. Often, a $70 faucet or cabinets that have been revived with a new coat of paint, create this appealing quality every bit as much as more expensive upgrades would.

Regardless of the changes you make, your kitchen should be bright, appealing, and spotless. Everything must be in good working condition and show little, if any, wear and tear. Dowdy wallpaper and grime around the faucet spout are glaring symbols of age and can strip thousands off your home's perceived value, not to mention making this communal center a less pleasurable place to spend your personal time. A good, inexpensive first step is to revive the room with a fresh coat of light-colored paint. Then pick from among the other kitchen projects featured in this chapter.

Faucets & Sinks

The combination of kitchen sink and faucet serves as a key focal point in the kitchen, one that is directly linked to the perception of how sanitary the space is. A spotless sink and blemish-free faucet can add many times their real costs to the perceived value of the room.

A thorough cleaning is the first step in updating your sink and faucet. Start by removing any rust and stains. Once clean, you can polish a stainless steel sink with a commercial polish to bring back the shine. You'll also want to make sure the faucet is in tip-top shape by repairing any drips or leaks. Most faucet repairs are easy if you have the right parts and you pay close attention to how the faucet is assembled while you're taking it apart. Take this opportunity to clean and repair the sprayer attachment as well. But if the faucet is cracked, pitted, or can't be repaired, you're better off replacing it. The same goes for your sink if it is noticeably chipped, discolored, or simply too beat up to be brought back to life with a thorough cleaning.

When buying a faucet, choose a decent-quality model that complements the sink and fits the style of the kitchen. The cheapest faucets can be had for less than $50, but these scream "rental property" and ruin this easy opportunity to add a touch of quality. You'll find much more stylish units, and a much wider selection, in the $70 to $90 range. Faucets with a single, lever-type handle are best for the kitchen because they allow you to turn on the water with your elbow or arm when your hands are covered with cookie dough. Keep in mind that the faucet you select must match the holes in the sink you're using. Most have four holes: three for the faucet and one for the sprayer (or you can use it for the dishwasher air gap or a soap dispenser).

A budget-minded sink replacement means you'll be shopping for a stainless steel or acrylic sink. Stainless steel is the standard and most popular choice among homeowners, primarily because the look complements a wide range of kitchen styles and the sink itself won't chip, stain, or fade. The price and quality of stainless steel sinks are linked to the thickness of the metal, the finish, and the overall look. Budget sinks (around $50) are made with 20-gauge or thinner steel and may or may not have sound-deadening material on the hidden outer sides of the basins. It's well worth upgrading to a thicker, 19-gauge or 18-gauge sink with some sound-deadening features. These are more dent-resistant and don't sound quite as hollow and flimsy when you set dishes into the basins.

Acrylic sinks are the other option for homeowners looking to save money and create a fresh focal point in the kitchen. You'll find handsome models for between $85 and $100, in a variety of colors. Acrylic sinks are easy to handle because they are so lightweight. However, you have to be more careful with them; they are easily scratched and can even melt if a hot pan is set in the basin.

After

Few improvements will have a bigger, faster payback than replacing a kitchen sink or faucet showing signs of age and wear.

Before

Buying a repair kit for the specific model of faucet you own is usually a better solution than trying to purchase replacement parts individually.

A kitchen faucet with a single-lever handle is easy to install and is a perennially popular and timeless look.

Replacing a Kitchen Sink & Faucet

To remove the old sink, turn off the water supplies at the shut-off valves, then disconnect the flexible risers (supply tubes) from the faucet tubes. Unscrew the sprayer hose from the faucet and remove the sprayer mount, if necessary.

Unplug the garbage disposer (if there is one), then disassemble the drain pieces by loosening the slip nuts on the pipes. The P-trap (the curved piece of pipe at the bottom of the drain assembly) is full of smelly water, so have a bucket handy. Stuff a rag or plastic bag into the drainpipe extending from the wall to stop sewer gases from rising into the room. Remove the disposer motor by twisting the mounting ring (see pages 10 to 11).

Lightweight, self-rimming sinks (such as most stainless steel models) are secured to the countertop with mounting clips; loosen the clip bolts to remove the clips or twist them to the side. Enameled cast iron sinks are typically held in place by their weight. Cut any caulking along the sink rim, then pull the sink up and out of the countertop.

Remove the strainer basket and garbage disposer's mounting assembly from the old sink (you might want to buy a new strainer basket, for looks). Test fit the new sink into the countertop hole, and make any necessary adjustments.

Added-Value Faucets

Don't have a sprayer attachment for your sink? Add one the easy way by selecting a replacement faucet with a pull-down or pull-out head. These units start at around $85 and come in a range of styles, from contemporary versions with a sleek pull-out head to dramatic gooseneck models featuring a pull-down sprayer bulb. Be sure that the sprayer hose is long enough to accommodate the size of your sink and the items you regularly clean in the sink.

The flowing neck of this stylish, modern faucet conceals a large, pull-out spray head that comes in handy for cleaning larger pots and pans.

● How to Replace a Kitchen Sink & Faucet

1 **Lay a bead of plumber's putty** along the recessed edge of each basin hole and under the faucet (if it wasn't sold with a plastic or rubber gasket). Mount the faucet, sink strainer, and disposer assembly before installing the sink.

2 **After lining up the new sink,** set it into a bead of silicone caulk laid on the countertop under the sink edge. Secure the sink with the new mounting brackets, following the manufacturer's directions.

3 **Hook up the water supply** and drain lines. It's usually worth spending a few dollars to install new supply risers from the stop valves to the faucet, and a new drain kit. Open the water valves and run the water and disposer to check for leaks.

Installing a Garbage Disposer

Garbage disposers are widely available at home stores in a range of sizes. For a primary kitchen sink, choose a model with a ½-horsepower or better motor (look to spend $70 to $100). Most building codes require that disposers be plugged into a dedicated GFCI receptacle controlled by a switch. The switch is typically mounted on the wall within reach of the sink faucet. If you don't have a receptacle, hire an electrician to install one.

Disposers are easy to install and come with most of the supplies you need to mount the unit to the sink. However, you might have to buy an appliance cord, wire nuts, and drain connections (including a strainer replacement with cover flaps). In a typical installation, the disposer's drain connects to a T-fitting on the vertical drainpipe coming down from the other sink basin. Disposer units include a nipple for connecting a dishwasher drain hose directly to the disposer. If you use this, be sure to remove the knockout inside the nipple before attaching the drain hose.

The installation process is described on the opposite page, but it's important to point out that making a secure electrical connection is simple yet essential. Remove the coverplate on the bottom of the motor unit to access the wiring. Connect an approved appliance cord following the manufacturer's wiring diagram, then reattach the coverplate.

Finish up by holding the motor unit in place and tightening the mounting ring by cranking on any accessible mounting lug, using a screwdriver. Twist the ring until it stops. Plug in the disposer, then run the water and disposer to check for leaks.

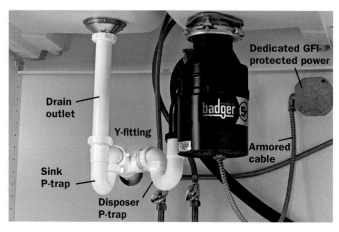

A properly functioning garbage disposer, used correctly, can actually help reduce clogs by ensuring that large bits of organic matter don't get into the drain system by accident. Many plumbers suggest using separate P-traps for the disposer and the drain outlet tube, as shown here.

Extending Disposer Life

Garbage disposers are subject to a lot of abuse; keeping the blades and chopping mechanism clean will not only help avoid nasty smells, it will stretch your appliance dollar by helping to increase the life of this workhorse. Once a month, grind a load of ice cubes and lemon peels with a couple tablespoons of baking soda. Then flush the disposer with a quart of boiling water and the unit will be as clean and fresh as when it was new.

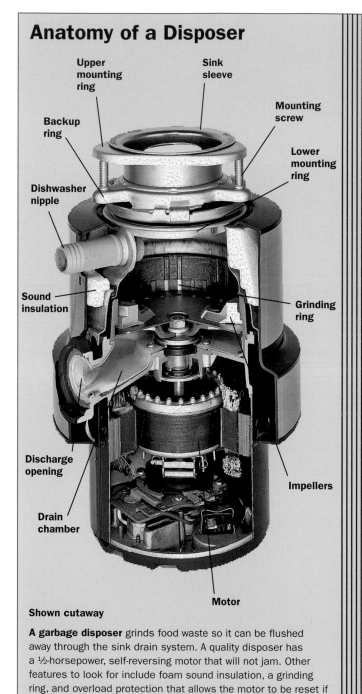

Anatomy of a Disposer

Upper mounting ring
Sink sleeve
Mounting screw
Backup ring
Lower mounting ring
Dishwasher nipple
Sound insulation
Grinding ring
Discharge opening
Impellers
Drain chamber
Motor

Shown cutaway

A garbage disposer grinds food waste so it can be flushed away through the sink drain system. A quality disposer has a ½-horsepower, self-reversing motor that will not jam. Other features to look for include foam sound insulation, a grinding ring, and overload protection that allows the motor to be reset if it overheats.

How to Install a Garbage Disposer

Sink sleeve

1 **Install the sink sleeve** and mounting assembly into the sink hole. A good seal with plumber's putty is critical to prevent leaks. From below, attach the mounting rings and snap ring to the sink sleeve (inset photo).

2 **Hang the motor unit** from the lower mounting ring, then assemble the drain pieces. The disposer may have an adjustable discharge tube to accommodate various configurations.

Dishwasher discharge tube

3 **Make the hookups** for the discharge tubes and the power cord. Once everything is lined up properly—with a ¼" per foot slope on horizontal drain pipes—tighten all of the slip nuts.

The Appliance Question

The required set of fixtures for any modern kitchen includes four appliances: refrigerator/freezer, range (or oven and cooktop), dishwasher, and garbage disposer. If your kitchen is missing any of these, it's time to get one. Most people also consider microwaves essential, but they fall into the category of portable appliances, so there's no need to have one if you're selling your house.

The first question entertained by many sellers and new homeowners is, "Should I replace the kitchen appliances?" This is a judgment call, and your real estate agent can advise you on what's best for your house and the local market if you're selling. If you're fixing up a house for sale, stick with this rule: If it ain't broke, don't replace it. Appliances must be clean and in good condition so buyers can use them right away when they move in. If you're a new homeowner and will be using the appliances for the next decade or so, consider energy efficiency when choosing new appliances. This is especially important with refrigerators. An inefficient, low-quality fridge will cost you a lot more in the long run due to the higher operating costs reflected in your electricity bill. An energy-efficient, no-frills fridge with the freezer on top is always a good option.

An appliance that works well and looks decent usually needs only a thorough cleaning to get it ready for a sale. From a resale standpoint, buying fancy new appliances seldom pays off in the sale price.

◖▮◗ Cabinets & Countertops

As the dominant elements in any kitchen, cabinets and countertop call for close attention. Cabinets make an instant impression, so a quick cosmetic makeover can do wonders. Although high-end conveniences, like slide-out shelves, custom corner units, or built-ins for appliances can add to the perceived value, the cabinet bodies and doors make the most impact on potential buyers and residents alike. Focus your attention on the overall look, specifically with the doors and drawer fronts, the cabinet faces, and the hardware. A typical quick makeover might involve cleaning or painting the outsides of the cabinets and replacing the knobs and pulls, as well as the hinges if they're visible and showing signs of wear.

Refacing cabinets involves covering visible cabinet surfaces with thin laminate or wood veneers and replacing the doors and drawer fronts. Although this is often touted as an option to new cabinetry, the truth is, it usually takes a pro to create an attractive refacing job without obvious blemishes. And the cost can often run $3,000 or more, so the benefit to resale or increased value of the home is negligible. Simple painting the cabinets is usually a better option.

A fresh look on the countertop is equally important. This is one of those places where traces of past use leave an unsavory feeling about the space. A buyer doesn't want to see the burn mark where you set a hot pan onto your laminate top. And if you've just moved into a house, you don't want to have to think about sanitizing the stained grout joints on a tiled surface.

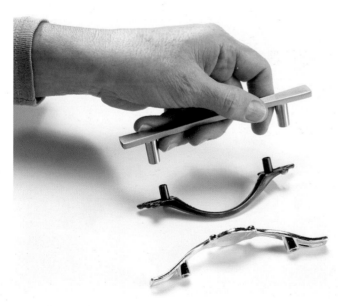

Replacing handles and pulls with clean, stylish hardware is one of the quickest and cheapest ways to freshen up old kitchen cabinets and drawers. *Tip: Bring your old hardware with you to the store to make sure the new hardware will fit the holes in your cabinets.*

A Low-Cost Luxury Upgrade

Glass-fronted cabinet doors are a stunning addition to any kitchen, but they add considerable cost to new cabinets. Skip the pricey new models and retrofit recessed-panel cabinet doors for the modest cost of a few pieces of glass. (Consider using colored or machined glass if you prefer to conceal what's inside the cabinet!)

Cut a recess for a glass panel in the frame. Use a router with a straight bit to cut away the lip on the rails and stiles of the door that holds the panel in place. Set the router to the depth of the lip. Clamp the door to the worksurface. Clamp guides to the worksurface. Rout out the lip. Remove the panel. Square the corners of the cutout with a chisel.

Install the glass. Measure the cutout and order a piece of tempered glass to fit. Consider the many types of glass, including colored, frosted, or pebbled, to coordinate with the rest of the kitchen and conceal the interior as desired. Use glass clips to install the panel. Reattach the hardware and rehang the door.

Kitchen Color

With their complex mix of shapes and materials, kitchens are quite busy to the eye. And while certain contrasts can be nice, such as pairing white cabinets with wood floors, starkly contrasting colors on the walls, cabinets, and counter surfaces tend to crowd the space with a hodgepodge of tones. When choosing colors for paint, tile, counters, and even appliances, go with complementary colors and always try to visualize the room as a whole. If you're selling your house, neutral tones are safer than bold color schemes. Just be sure to include some accents of color or texture to prevent a bland or sterile atmosphere.

For painted cabinets, white, neutral, and natural colors are safe choices because they recede, making the space appear larger. They also convey a positive message: clean and fresh. Use walls and decorative accents to add splashes of color to the space.

Painting Cabinets

If your painted cabinets need refreshing, or if your wood-finish cabinets are unattractive, a careful DIY paint job will quickly bring them back to life. For a little more money, you can opt to have the cabinets professionally spray-painted (look in the phone book under Painting Contractors, and find someone with experience in cabinet work).

High-quality, lasting results require a lot of prep work. Clean all surfaces to be painted with trisodium phosphate (TSP). This removes greasy buildup and slightly etches the surface to help the new paint to adhere.

An alkyd or acrylic latex primer is appropriate for most jobs. But if the cabinets are badly stained or there are any exposed wood knots, prime the surfaces with a shellac-base sealer to prevent problem areas from bleeding through the topcoats. After the primer dries, lightly sand the surface if necessary for a smooth finish.

Always apply paint to cabinets with a high quality brush, not a roller (which leaves stipple marks) or foam applicator. You might be surprised at how much a good brush costs, but the better results and ease-of-use are undeniable. If you clean the brush carefully after each use, it will serve you well for years. Use a natural-bristle brush for alkyd paint and a nylon-bristle brush for latex.

Apply the topcoats of paint in this order: For raised-panel doors, paint the panel first, the horizontal rails next, and the vertical stiles last. Paint both sides of the door, and use long, smooth stokes to prevent brush marks. Paint drawer fronts along the edges first, then along the front faces. If you're painting the insides of the cabinets, do the back panel first, then the top, the sides, and the bottom last. Finally, paint the face frames of the cabinet boxes, starting with the verticals and finishing with the horizontals. You'll probably need at least two topcoats (plus the primer) for a solid finish.

The Best Value in Paint

Both latex (water-based) and alkyd (oil-based) paints work well on cabinets. Latex cleans up easily and gives off fewer noxious fumes. However, many pros still prefer alkyd paints for cabinets and other woodwork, arguing that these types provide a tougher, smoother finish that hides brush strokes better than latex paints. It's your call. If you use latex, choose a 100 percent acrylic formulation, which sticks better and is more durable than vinyl acrylic. Spend more for a name-brand paint, because bargain brands tend to cover poorly and will deteriorate more quickly—costing you more in the long run. In all cases, opt for gloss sheen (not semi-gloss, eggshell, or flat) for greater durability and washability.

Refinishing Hardwood Cabinets

For nicer cabinets made of an attractive hardwood, such as maple, cherry, or walnut, painting would be downright sacrilegious and a huge missed opportunity. Like hardwood floors, there's too much value in the material to justify covering it up for convenience. Solid-wood cabinets with a good finish can often be renewed with a thorough cleaning and polishing. You might need something strong to remove the old layers of cooking grime. A solution of mineral spirits is often recommended for some cabinets and furniture, or a commercial wood cleaner might do the trick. Just make sure whatever you use doesn't scratch, dull, or remove the wood's finish.

Refinishing hardwood cabinets is a messy, laborious job, but it can be well worth the effort with nice cabinetry. If you're up to this task, ask your local home center representative to lead you to the best products for stripping the old finish. Expect to do a lot of sanding as well, to bring the wood back to its original state. Although staining takes some practice and know-how, applying a clear protective finish is easy. Most types of wood will look great with three coats of clear polyurethane. A popular brand of wipe-on polyurethane is easy to work with and gives the finish more of a hand-rubbed look than the thick, glossy finish used on hardwood flooring.

Refinishing hardwood cabinets? For ease of application and practically guaranteed success, try using a wipe-on polyurethane topcoat product.

How to Paint Cabinets

Remove doors and drawers for better access, including hinges and all other hardware. Thoroughly clean all the surfaces and then give everything a light sanding with 150-grit sandpaper to rough up the surface and provide tooth for the paint.

Fill all holes and dents with a non-shrinking wood putty, let it dry, and sand the area smooth. Prime the cabinets, doors, and drawer fronts. Paint the doors and face frames with enamel paint. Two or three light coats will provide a better, more durable appearance than one thick coat.

Don't forget about the interiors. A coat of fresh light-colored paint will make dreary cabinets feel new. Be careful not to clog shelf-hanger holes on the inside, and paint the shelves if they are the same material as the cabinet boxes.

Let the final coat dry for several days before reinstalling doors and hardware, to prevent sticking. Rehang the doors and attach new or revitalized hardware. You'll be amazed by how fresh and stylish newly painted cabinets look.

Slide-out Storage

Slide-out kitchen shelf drawers scream custom kitchen even though they are an incredibly simple upgrade to existing cabinetry. Not only are these types of storage extremely useful, they also click with prospective buyers, instilling the impression that your kitchen is modern, well-appointed, and user-friendly.

There are many different types of slide-out units to choose from. Basic shelves come with or without sides and a back, and start at about $35 per shelf (all prices include the slide sets). Boxes are often handier for keeping loose items in order, and these run from $40 to over $70, depending on the size and material used to construct the box. You can also find specialized slide-out or pull-out units, such as spice racks (ideal for very skinny spaces between cabinets where traditional shelving would look odd) and swing-up or swing-out shelves that can be used as temporary counter space for appliances such as a blender.

All of these share simple and easy installation. If you have a level, a screwdriver, a drill, and 20 minutes, you've got everything you need to make a kitchen cabinet more functional for you or fancier for the buyer looking to purchase a home with an updated kitchen.

Wise Buys in Slide-out Storage

When it comes to buying slide-out storage units, save money by installing them in a standard-width cabinet. Stock slide-out trays and shelves are sized to fit traditional widths of cabinets. If you want to install movable shelves or drawers in an odd-size cabinet, you'll need to wait longer and pay more for a custom order—usually $10 to $15 extra per shelf.

Slide-out trays are easy to install, great storage options, and add to the perceived value and style of your kitchen. Consider what you need to store before deciding on where to position shelves or trays within the cabinet.

Drawer Slides

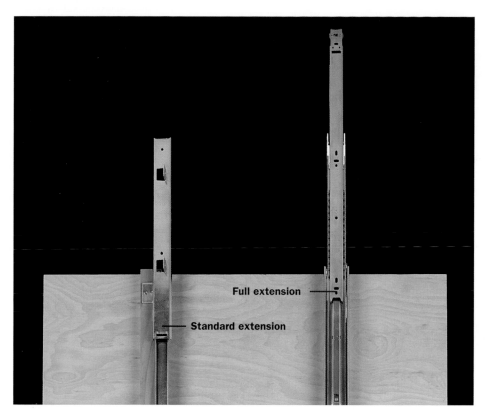

Drawer slides suitable for pullout shelves are commonly available in both standard (left) and full extension (right) styles. Standard slides are less expensive and good enough for most applications. They allow the tray to be pulled out most of the way. Full extension slides are a little pricier than standard slides but they allow the tray to be pulled completely out of the cabinet box for easy access to items in the back.

Full extension

Standard extension

Installing Slide-out Storage

Slide-out shelves or trays are exceptionally easy to install. Simply mark where you want the unit positioned and use wood screws to attach a 1 × 3 spacer in the cabinet as shown, checking level as you go. Screw the slide to the spacer ensuring that it is level as well. Then simply push the slide on the tray or shelf into the slide you've mounted, and you're done!

Quick Fixes for Old Countertops

If you think about it, we ask a lot of our kitchen counters. One moment we treat them with about as much care as a garage workbench, and then we expect them to shine like new with just a quick wipe-up. If your countertop is starting to show more of the beating and less of the shine, it's time to take a hard look at the situation and consider your options for upgrades. Often, a creative solution will allow you to salvage an old counter that's in decent shape, so you can move on to your next project with your budget intact. Here, we'll look at fixes for the two very common types of countertops (laminate and tile) along with some tips for repairing and renewing solid-surface materials.

Laminate Countertops

Laminate is the most popular type of kitchen work surface because it is a versatile and inexpensive material. The plastic compounds used to make laminate surfaces ensure that the countertops are stain-resistant, durable, and sanitary. It's also maintenance-free, requiring only regular cleaning. If you don't turn up your nose at the look of laminate, its only real drawbacks are that it's susceptible to damage.

Topping the list of common laminate damage problems are knife marks, burns, delamination and misaligned or curling seams. While damaged laminate isn't exactly fixable and you can't make scars disappear, there are some simple repairs you can make to spruce up your laminate.

Did someone forget to use a cutting board? You can help hide scratches and light gouges in laminate with a commercial seam filler, available from laminate manufacturers. For chips or small holes, you can purchase a repair kit from home and hardware stores. Seam filler and repair kits consist of a plastic compound that you mix to match the color of your surface. Follow the product directions for mixing and applying the patch. Again, the repair won't be invisible, but it's better than doing nothing.

Burn marks are next on the list, as many a laminate countertop has been marred by a hot pan, a fallen cigarette, or a pot holder left too close to a stovetop burner. If the burn is near a cooking area, you're in luck; you can cut out the damage and set a large tile into the surface to create a built-in trivet (see page 19).

Because a laminate countertop is made from a thin sheet of resin paper and plastic glued to a wood substrate, the laminate layer sometimes peels up or even bubbles in spots.

This is usually the result of a poor glue job or a hot object being set onto the surface. To reattach peeling laminate, lift it up as far as you can, carefully scrape off the old glue (usually contact cement), then reapply new contact cement to both surfaces and let it dry, following the product directions. Bond the laminate back to the substrate using a J-roller. Roll the laminate by working out from the fixed end, to prevent trapping air underneath and creating a bubble. Once the laminate is stuck, the job is done.

When it comes to failing seams, large-scale delamination and other signs of water damage, there's really no fix other than complete replacement. Laminate itself is impervious to water, but the particleboard substrate soaks it up like a roll of paper towels, and expands pretty much the same way. Once this happens, you can't get the board flat again. Good carpenters and installers know about the importance of keeping countertop seams away from sinks, for this very reason.

Seam filling compound (see Resources, page 140) is purchased pre-tinted to match common plastic laminate colors. It can be used to repair minor chips and scratches or to fill separated seams between laminate sheets.

A vinyl and leather repair kit (see Resources, page 140) can be used for touch-up repairs on laminate countertops. The kits are widely available for around $10, and are simple to use. Prepare the repair area with an abrasive pad, blend paints to achieve similar color, apply the paint, cover with a clear coat ad then heat-set with a household iron after the paint dries.

A Low-cost Luxury Look

You want to add value to the kitchen but you want to stay within your budget. You can do both by replacing a timeworn or damaged island laminate countertop or breakfast bar with tile. Use a tile that complements the other laminate countertop surfaces and you'll create an expensive look for a fraction of the cost of tiling all the countertops—in most cases less than $5 per square foot.

Turning Damage into a Focal Point

Replace a small section of damaged laminate near a stove with a tile trivet insert. This requires a router, a mortising bit with a top-mounted guide bearing, a scrap of plywood, a tile saw, and some heat-resistant caulk.

To make the repair, trace the tile outline onto the wood scrap, then carefully cut along the line with a saw. This creates a template for the router bit to follow. Ideally, the cutout should be about 1/16 inch larger than the tile in each direction. Secure the template to the countertop using clamps or dabs of hot glue. Rout out the laminate and cut into the substrate to a depth that's slightly shallower than the thickness of the tile. The tile should stand a little proud of the countertop so you can set a pan onto the tile without touching the surrounding laminate. Glue the tile in place with the caulk, then caulk along the edges of the tile to create a watertight seal with the laminate.

You can use an understated tile as shown here or, if you want to make more of a splash, opt for something a little more interesting. For less than $20, you can choose a hand-painted tile, a quarry stone tile, or pick from any of the more exotic choices such as glass or steel.

Flatten a bubble in laminate by heating with an iron and then rolling with a J-roller to re-bond the laminate to its substrate. Use a towel to prevent the iron from scorching the laminate, and set the iron on low to medium heat. Keep rolling until the surface cools.

Replacing Laminate & Postform Countertops

Your options for making more extensive fixes than simple crack-and-dent repairs depend largely on what kind of countertop you have. Postform countertops are factory-made surfaces with one continuous layer of laminate from the top of the backsplash to the front edge of the counter. They have a raised, bullnosed front edge to help contain spills without hindering cleanup. This makes postform counters difficult to modify with upgrades. You can't cover them with new laminate because of the curves, and preparing the surface for tile requires so much demolition and modification that you might be better off starting from scratch with a new plywood substrate.

Custom laminate counters are usually flat across the top and may have custom add-ons, like wood trim along the front edge, a square laminate backsplash, or a tile backsplash. Your custom countertop was probably created by one of the professionals who built your house. Working with laminate is a cinch for a skilled builder, and custom countertops allow you to cover large expanses without seams, creating any shape desired (postform tops are available only in straight sections).

A flat custom countertop is more adaptable than a postform top. You can apply a new layer of laminate, add a hardwood edge, or remove the old backsplash and tile a new one. Covering the old top with a new layer of laminate is a big job, but it's a relatively cheap and easy way to get a new countertop.

If your postform laminate counter is in very bad shape, consider replacing it with exactly the same thing in a new laminate. You can buy straight and mitered (cut at a 90 degree angle, for corners) sections of postform tops at home centers and lumberyards in a limited range of colors. You can also order sections from a local fabricator. This costs more, but you'll have a bigger selection of colors and styles to choose from.

Best Tile Value

A tiled backsplash is a way for you to give your countertops a custom look with less than a day's work. Plain white 4 × 4 tiles run as little as $1.25 per square foot (add in a few pricier designer tiles to spruce up the look without breaking the bank), and stone tile such as the slate shown here can be found for around $4.50 per square foot. It's an easy project. Just set the tiles onto the wall with mastic or thin-set tile adhesive, leaving a slight gap at the bottom for a bead of silicone caulk. Grout and seal as you would a countertop or floor and you'll have an eye-catching feature that increases the value of your kitchen.

Ceramic wall tile makes an inexpensive, easy-to-install new backsplash, or an attractive replacement for an ugly backsplash, to give your countertop a fresh, custom-made appearance.

Add New Edging

Hardwood edging dresses up an old countertop nicely and is a good solution for a badly chipped or worn edge. Remove the old laminate edge strips and contact cement and carefully sand the edges of the subbase smooth. If the old laminate surface overhangs the edges, trim it with a laminate trimmer or router and a flush-cutting bit. Rip cut the edging to width from ¾"-thick stock. Secure the edging in place with water-resistant wood glue and finish nails, making sure the top of the edging is flush with the top of the countertop surface. Set the nails and fill the nails holes with tinted wood putty. Touch up the joints and nail holes with the finish you used on the edging.

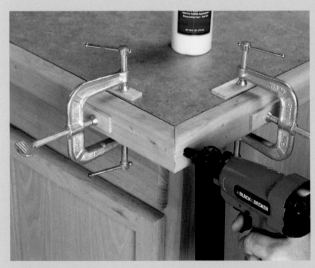

Add elegant hardwood edging to dress up a countertop that is showing edge wear.

How to Replace a Postform Countertop

1 **Remove the old countertop** by unscrewing it at the mounting tabs or corner blocks where it is attached. If possible, save the take-up bolts holding mitered corners together from underneath the top. Discard the old countertop.

2 **Cut the countertop sections to length,** as needed, sawing from the back side with a circular saw or jigsaw and a straightedge. Attach matching end caps to any ends that will be exposed, including ends that stop at an opening for a range or refrigerator.

3 **Set the countertop section into position** on the cabinet bases. Add buildup strips of particleboard or plywood as needed to make the bottom of the countertop flush and level with the top of the base cabinets. Test-fit the countertop to the wall, then scribe a line onto the backsplash using a pencil or compass. Remove the countertop and sand up to the scribed line with a belt sander.

4 **Join pre-mitered countertop sections in place,** using take-up bolts and sealing the joint with silicone sealant (left photo). Draw the miter together tightly with the take-up bolts set into the precut recesses on the undersides of the sections (right photo). Fasten the countertop to the cabinets and caulk along the backsplash and wall seam.

Tile Countertops

Ceramic or porcelain tile countertops are popular because they offer a custom look at a relatively low price. You'll find them in every color of the rainbow to match just about any kitchen decor, as well as more expensive, hand-painted styles. Even the granite craze has extended to tile, in the form of real granite tiles available at a fraction of the cost of solid-slab stone—starting at about $2 per square foot. Tiles are extremely durable, heat-resistant, and stain-resistant. The grout, however, stains easily, and its rough texture makes everyday cleaning a chore.

Over time, tiled countertops may crack and grout lines can crumble and stain. Fortunately, tile repairs are straightforward and effective. Even replacing a tile in the middle of a countertop, as shown on page 23, can be easily done with basic tools and no particular skill.

Cleaning and re-sealing the grout can work small miracles on your countertop, provided the tiles are in good shape. Recommended cleaning solutions vary from mild household products, like vinegar or baking soda, to heavy-duty commercial grout cleaners. Vinegar is good for water deposits but not so effective with food stains. It can also discolor some grouts. One of the best things to try first is oxygen bleach, available in powder form that you mix with water according to the directions. Oxygen bleach is nontoxic and won't cause colors to fade as standard chemical bleaches do. Apply the solution liberally to the grout and wait 30 to 60 minutes, then scrub the joints with a stiff nylon grout brush, working in tight circles. Rinse thoroughly and seal the grout with a food-safe grout sealer.

If your grout simply won't come clean or is badly worn in many places, you probably need to regrout. This is a painstaking process, but it is effective. See pages 50 to 51 for a discussion of how to replace grout.

Oxygen bleach is less caustic than standard chlorine bleach and can be used to clean grout lines without fear of affecting the color of the surrounding tile.

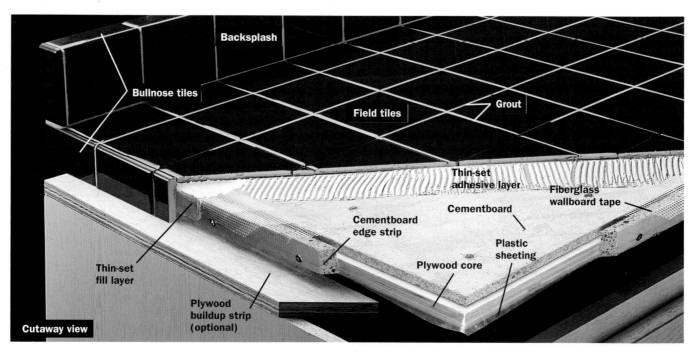

Backsplash

Bullnose tiles

Field tiles

Grout

Thin-set adhesive layer

Fiberglass wallboard tape

Cementboard edge strip

Cementboard

Plastic sheeting

Plywood core

Thin-set fill layer

Plywood buildup strip (optional)

Cutaway view

A ceramic tile countertop made with wall tile starts with a core of ¾" exterior-grade plywood that's covered with a moisture barrier of 4-mil polyethylene sheeting. Half-inch cementboard is screwed to the plywood, and the edges are capped with cementboard and finished with fiberglass mesh tape and thin-set mortar. Tiles for edging and backsplashes may be bullnose or trimmed from the factory edges of field tiles.

How to Replace a Countertop Tile

1 **Use a cold chisel** to remove fragments of broken ceramic tiles. Always direct the chisel away from the surrounding tiles to prevent damaging them. Clean up the old grout and mortar or adhesive with a sharp paint scraper.

2 **Replace broken countertop tiles** with matching new ones. Apply enough adhesive to the bottom of the new tile so the top will sit flush with the surrounding tiles. If you do not have any leftover tiles from the countertop installation, you can probably find a near-match at a well-stocked tile store. Replace grout around the tile after the adhesive sets.

Cleaning Up Solid-Surface Countertops

Solid-surface countertops are composed of the same material through and through, which makes them almost totally renewable. Cleaning and repair methods vary by manufacturer, so whenever possible contact the maker of your countertop for detailed recommendations. Here are some of the basic solutions for the most common brands:

- **Fine scratches and blotches:** Apply a mild abrasive cleanser to the area, then rub in a circular motion with a damp sponge or cloth. Work from front to back, then side-to-side. Rinse thoroughly and wipe dry.
- **Minor cuts:** Wash the area with soapy water or an ammonia-based cleaner (not window cleaner). Leave the surface wet and rub lightly with an abrasive pad, working in a line parallel to the scratch, then perpendicularly until the cut is gone. If the scrubbed area is visible after the surface dries, blend the areas by scrubbing with progressively finer pads to restore the original finish.
- **Burn marks and deep cuts:** If the above solutions do not work, sand out the damage with fine sandpaper. Blend the repair area and restore the finish by following the solutions above.
- **Cracks and other extensive damage:** It can be expensive, but solid-surface fabricators can fix pretty much anything. Call around to find some good local pros and compare pricing. Fabricators can also completely restore a countertop finish to its original luster.

Buff out light scratches in solid-surface material with a mild abrasive cleanser and nonmetallic abrasive pad.

Fine sandpaper can be used to buff deep defects from solid-surface countertops, but try less aggressive solutions first.

Flooring Repairs & Upgrades

A kitchen floor is generally judged on two counts: how it looks and how much maintenance it needs. If you're selling the house, your kitchen floor should look more or less new. As with countertops, old scars and stains on a floor are not only unsightly but can also be unsanitary. If you think it might be time to replace your kitchen floor, consider installing sheet vinyl, vinyl tiles, or laminate planks. These all rank near the bottom of the price scale and are right at the top of the low-maintenance list.

A kitchen floor that is out of date, in poor repair, or both is an instant turnoff to new homeowners and potential buyers alike.

Vinyl Flooring Fixes

Vinyl flooring is the most popular type of resilient flooring (flat-surface flooring that is soft underfoot) thanks to its relatively low cost, superb water and stain resistance, and excellent durability. It's also one of the easiest and cheapest types of flooring to install.

There are two types of vinyl flooring: sheet vinyl, which comes in big rolls and is (ideally) laid in one continuous piece, and vinyl tiles or planks—individual pieces laid in a pattern and stuck to the subfloor with glue or self-adhesive backing. Sheet vinyl runs between $.50 and $5 per square foot, depending on thickness, construction, and complexity of the design. Vinyl tiles and planks range between $.25 and $4.50 per square foot, depending on those same factors.

Linoleum is another well-known resilient flooring. It has been around since the late 1800s and is an all-natural product, made with linseed oil, sawdust, cork, and other organic materials. Real linoleum has the right qualities for the kitchen and is now available in a range of appealing colors and patterns, but installing sheet linoleum is a job for professionals. Plank and tile linoleum are similar in price to vinyl and are DIY-friendly, but vinyl remains the most popular flooring for its all-around excellent characteristics.

Sheet vinyl is more durable and has a higher quality look than most vinyl tiles. This is because the seams in tile can be gathering places for dirt and grime, and can allow water to infiltrate and compromise the adhesive bond between tile and floor. The main advantage, however, is that individual tiles are easy to replace and the initial installation is also easier. Damaged sheet vinyl can be patched, but not without leaving visible seams. Vinyl tiles can loosen at the edges and curl up, but you can simply replace the affected pieces. Repairs for both conditions are shown on page 25. Ideally, you or the previous owner had the foresight to save extra tiles for this purpose. If not, bring a sample of the flooring with you to local flooring stores to see if they can match it. *Note: Older floor tiles and adhesive may contain asbestos. If you suspect your flooring was made or installed before 1980, consult the U.S. EPA recommendations for asbestos in the home, available online at www.epa.gov.*

Bargain Adhesive

When it comes to saving money long term, bargain tile adhesives are really no bargain at all. Spend a few dollars more for the adhesive recommended by the tile manufacturer and you'll protect against eventual adhesive failure, bleed-through, and other problems that can occur with off-brand adhesives.

How to Replace a Vinyl Tile

1 **Heat the damaged tile** with a heat gun set on low or medium, or an iron on top of a dishtowel. When the tile and adhesive are soft enough, pry up the tile with a putty knife or a 5-in-1 painter's tool. Let the adhesive cool and harden, then scrape it up so that the underlayment is clean and smooth.

2 **Fill holes and depressions** in the subfloor with floor patching compound. Apply tile adhesive to the clean subfloor, using a notched trowel. Set the new tile in place and press it flat. If necessary, add or remove adhesive so that the tile is flush with the neighboring tiles.

3 **Roll the replacement tile** with a J-roller, working from the center of the tile toward the seams to avoid trapping air bubbles. Clean up any excess glue that squeezes out at the seams. Let the adhesive cure completely before walking on the tile.

Tip

You don't have to replace a tile that is just curling at one edge. Heat the affected area with a heat gun until tile and adhesive are soft. Carefully pull up the loose edge and scrape out the old adhesive and any accumulated dirt. Use a putty knife to apply vinyl tile adhesive to the back side of the tile, then press the tile back into place. Clean up any excess adhesive from the edges following the manufacturer's directions. Roll with a J-roller and place a weight on the tile until the adhesive cures completely.

Sheet Vinyl Floors

You can make passable (but not seamless) spot repairs to sheet vinyl flooring by patching in pieces of the same material. Patches are easiest to hide on flooring that has a pattern with faux grout joints or decorative grid lines—the dark lines help hide the seams of the patch. But if the entire floor is in bad shape, consider replacing it.

To patch a damaged area, cut an oversize scrap piece of flooring large enough to overlap all pattern lines surrounding the patch area (use the same material as the old flooring or the patch will be too conspicuous). Clean the floor thoroughly before putting the patch in place. You'll want to be careful in positioning the patch—the more exactly it's aligned, the more invisible the patch will be. Always use a straightedge for cutting the patch, for this same reason.

Depending on the original installation, the flooring may or may not be glued to the subfloor in all areas. Try to remove the cutout section. If it won't come up, that means it is set in adhesive, which will need to be softened for removal. When cleaning out the leftover adhesive, it may help to blot the area with mineral spirits or an adhesive remover.

Finish up by setting the new tile in place as shown below. Be sure to use seam sealer, because it helps hide the seam and creates a watertight seal to protect the subfloor.

Ceramic Tile Substitute

If you're replacing a vinyl floor in a bathroom or kitchen to prepare the home for sale, consider spending a little more ($.50 to $1 per sq. ft.) on an embossed vinyl that creates the look of actual tile. The value perception will be much higher than a flat vinyl, and the surface relief makes for a much more interesting floor. Embossed vinyl flooring is also thicker than most flat vinyls, making it more durable and a better investment over the long run. If you want to create the look of wood floors with far less expense, turn to contemporary photo reproduction sheet vinyls that present a very realistic wood appearance with the characteristic soft feel underfoot.

This embossed sheet vinyl flooring looks convincingly like elegant tile, but with a warm, soft feel underfoot.

● How to Patch Sheet Vinyl

1 **Align the patch** with the pattern on the existing flooring, then double-cut through both the patch and the floor covering, following the pattern lines for perfectly matched seams.

2 **Use a heat gun** set on medium or low to soften the adhesive and remove the cut sheet vinyl section from the cutout area. Clean up the underlayment with a floor scraper.

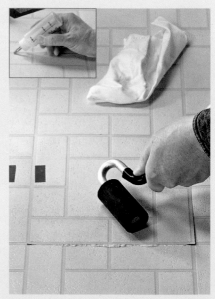

3 **Glue the new patch** into the cutout area with flooring adhesive. Roll with a J-roller to secure the patch. Once the patch adhesive has cured, carefully fill the seams around the patch with a commercial seam-sealing compound (inset).

Installing Sheet Vinyl Flooring

Replacing ugly, old vinyl flooring with new sheet vinyl is a fairly easy upgrade with a lot of bang for your buck. If the old floor covering is smooth, flat, and well adhered, you can get by with laying the new flooring over the old. However, it's always better to remove the old floor first. After removing the flooring, scrape off any leftover adhesive with a floor scraper. The floor must be smooth and clean before laying new vinyl. If the surface is rough or has exposed imperfections, add an underlayment (usually ¼" plywood) to create a smooth surface for the flooring.

The easiest way to install sheet vinyl is the perimeter-bond method, wherein the sheet is secured only along the edges. Because sheet vinyl is available in rolls up to 12 feet wide, many kitchen floors can be covered with a single, seamless sheet.

Here are the basic steps to installing new sheet vinyl. Create a cutting template with 15-pound building paper (roofing felt). Join cut sections with duct tape, and adhere the template to the floor by cutting boat-shaped holes and taping over the holes with duct tape. Trim the template along the edges to follow obstructions. Trim right up to obstructions.

Roll out the new flooring face-up, and let it warm up for a while so it lies flat. Place the template over the flooring (the tape over the boat-shaped holes keeps the template in place). Score along the template edges (or use a straightedge to compensate for the scribe offset) to mark the cutting lines onto the new flooring. Then, cut the flooring all the way through with a hooked blade on the utility knife or linoleum knife.

Roll up the vinyl bottom side out, and set it into place for a test-fit. Make any necessary adjustments to the cuts and bond the flooring with a three-inch-wide strip of flooring adhesive along the perimeter (or as directed by the flooring manufacturer). Roll the flooring flat with a floor roller. Cover the edges with baseboard and/or shoe molding.

Working with Templates

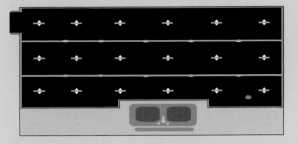

Make a cutting template for a single piece of sheet vinyl flooring using building paper. Cutouts made at regular intervals and crossed with a strip of duct tape keep the template stuck to the floor while you trim or mark the template.

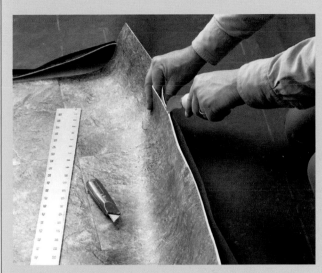

With the new flooring laying face-up on a flat surface, position the template on the flooring and tape it down. Score along the cutting lines with a utility knife and straightedge to about one-third of the flooring's depth (don't cut all the way through). Use a flooring knife with a hooked blade to complete the cuts.

Alternatives for the Kitchen

Tile is a classic kitchen flooring for its durability and water-resistance. The appearance is considered a big step up from vinyl flooring. But the price can be prohibitive ranging from about $1.50 to more than $20 per sq. ft. before installation. And if you have tile in your kitchen, you already know that the grout is susceptible to staining and dirt buildup. Aside from replacing broken tiles (see page 23) or repairing damaged or missing grout (page 51), scouring the grout to restore its original coloring is the best quick fix for a tiled floor—and often the only repair needed. Follow the steps for cleaning grout on tile countertops (page 22), then apply a grout sealer to help prevent stains.

Laminate flooring is steadily gaining popularity for kitchen floors, thanks to its easy cleanup and better-than-average scratch and stain resistance. But it can be pricey ($3 to $5 per sq. ft.), and it's not as waterproof as sheet vinyl, or as damage resistant as ceramic tile. Newer types of laminate do, however, hold up under everyday kitchen use. As a replacement flooring, laminate is a good choice for fixer-uppers because it's fairly inexpensive and easy to install as a floating floor over a bare subfloor or any clean, flat, secure surface. See pages 74 to 75 for more information on laminate flooring.

⬤ Lighting

Unless a special fixture has caught your eye, there's no reason to spend the money on fancy new lighting in the kitchen. Lighting is very much a matter of personal taste. That said, if your kitchen is lit by a single, old overhead fixture, replacing it with something brighter and a little more stylish is a worthwhile upgrade that will make your kitchen a more pleasant room to work in. Because the ceiling underneath the old light base probably doesn't match the surrounding ceiling, you'd be smart to choose a new light that covers slightly more of the ceiling so you don't have to do any patching.

Another easy improvement is adding under-cabinet lighting. Mounted underneath wall cabinets to illuminate the counter surfaces, under-cabinet fixtures provide the best task lighting for work areas. With the overhead lighting off, they create a soft, indirect glow perfect for mealtimes and entertaining. Finally, for a much-needed decorative touch, you can add a set of pendant lights over the kitchen sink or an eat-in counter. An inexpensive pair or trio of pendant fixtures can be had for under $100.

Old light fixtures don't just look dated, they often provide poor illumination as well, making the entire kitchen look even more dim and dated. By doing a simple one-for-one swap out with an updated ceiling light, you can kill two birds with one stone by getting rid of the old fixture and making everything else in the room look better. Choose a new light with a slightly larger base than the old one.

Lighting on a Budget

If you're updating a ceiling fixture and would like to add pendants or other dispersed lighting—but don't want to foot the added expense—consider buying an overhead light with multiple directional heads. They are comparable in price to other ceiling fixtures, although they are offered in a more limited selection of styles (white and stainless steel are the most commonly available). However, these types of fixtures give you excellent control over what part off the kitchen is lit at any given time.

Pendant lights are all the rage these days. Depending on their location, they can serve as task lights and/or accent fixtures.

How to Replace an Overhead Kitchen Light

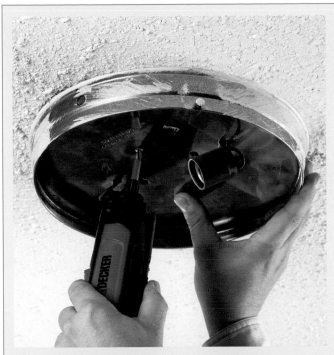

1 **Remove the old fixture.** First, shut off power to the light at the main service panel. Remove the globe or diffuser and the light bulbs in case you drop the fixture. Unscrew the mounting screws or nut holding the fixture to the ceiling box.

2 **Disconnect the old wires** after testing with a circuit tester to make sure the wires are not live. Inspect the wires in the ceiling to make sure they are in good repair. If you have more than 6" of wire on the inside of the fixture box in the ceiling, trim the ends and strip ½" of sheathing off each wire. If the sheathing is damaged in any way, replace it (contact an electrician for this job).

3 **Connect the wires to the new light.** Have a helper hold the light while you connect black to black and white to white using wire caps. Connect the ground wires and attach a short wire from both ground leads to the grounding terminal in the metal ceiling box.

4 **Hang the fixture base** using mounting screws or by tightening the mounting nut onto the threaded rod in the box. Install bulbs, restore power, and test the light. If it works, attach the diffuser lens or globe.

Installing Undercabinet Lights

The best all-around undercabinet lights are slim-line fluorescent fixtures that measure about 1⅛ inches thick and fit nicely into the recess areas at the bottoms of wall-hung cabinets. Fluorescent tubes are bright and energy-efficient, and they run much cooler than the popular halogen "puck" lights. Choose the right fixture size for each cabinet location, and make sure the lights can be wired in a series, so you need only connect one fixture to the power source.

You can power undercabinet lights with a direct connection to an appropriate kitchen circuit, or even tie them into the circuit that controls the overhead light, so one switch controls all of the room lights. However, the easiest installation method is to plug in the fixture using the provided power cord. A basic fluorescent plug-in fixture will run about $25 to $30.

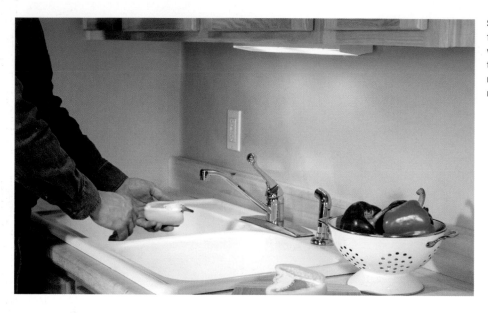

Slim-line compact fluorescent tube lights fit neatly in the recess underneath a wall cabinet. Power can be supplied through an existing light circuit, but do not tap into the dedicated small appliance receptacle circuit.

Adding a New Light Fixture

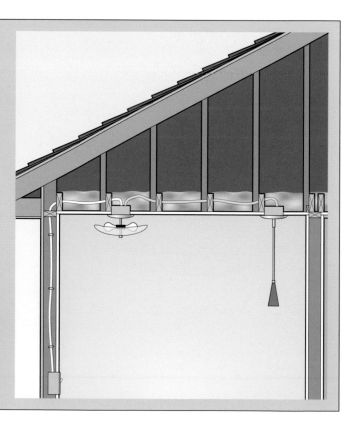

Installing a new fixture where none exists is easy if you have access to the kitchen ceiling from an open attic above. Without such access, you can still make the power connections as long as there's an open joist cavity between the existing overhead light and the new light (be sure to check with the local building department for code requirements on securing cable runs in this situation).

To install a new fixture, such as track lighting or an accent light, shut off the power at the main service panel and then cut a hole in the ceiling for a new ceiling box. Run the appropriate type of NM (nonmetallic) cable from the existing overhead light fixture box to the hole. Remove the overhead fixture, and connect the new cable to the circuit. Secure the cable to the ceiling framing, then install the remodel box.

Connect the new fixture according to the provided wiring diagram. To add one or two additional fixtures, follow the same procedure, running circuit cable from one fixture to the next (be sure the total power demand on the circuit does not exceed safe capacity).

If the circuit can accommodate it, you can branch from an existing overhead light to power the new fixtures and control them by the same wall switch.

Cleaning Kitchen Surfaces

CABINETS

Clean cabinet fronts with a cloth and appropriate cleaner, working from top to bottom. Rinse with a clean, water-dampened cloth to remove all cleaner residue. Wipe shelves with a slightly dampened cloth (water and dish soap); dry. Use appropriate polish for the hinges, pulls, and other hardware on cabinets and drawers.

CLEANERS FOR CABINET SURFACES

Natural wood: Use water and wood cleaner or dish soap and wipe with the grain. Dry, then buff horizontally with a clean cloth.

Painted wood: Use water and dish soap, but do a test sample first to check for discoloration.

Laminate: Use all-purpose cleaner sprayed onto a cloth and buff with a clean cloth.

Thermofoil (vinyl-clad): Use glass cleaner applied to cloth and buff with a clean cloth.

COUNTERTOPS

Laminate: Rub in a circular motion, using a moist sponge or soft nylon pad sprayed with all-purpose cleaner (abrasive cleansers and steel wool or stiff brushes can scratch laminate). Rinse with a water-dampened cloth.

Ceramic (glazed) or porcelain tile: Clean stained grout with oxygen bleach (see page 22) or other grout-bleaching stick. Wipe tile surfaces in a circular motion, using a cloth dipped in a solution of one capful of rubbing alcohol to one gallon of water.

Solid-surface (satin/matte finish): Wipe in a circular motion, using a cloth dampened with water and a small amount of dish soap. Buff with a clean cloth.

Butcher Block: Wipe with a cloth moistened with white vinegar to kill bacteria. Wipe along the grain with a cloth dampened with warm water and dish soap, wrung out. Rinse with a spray of clean water and wipe clean. Dry with a clean cloth.

SINK

Stainless steel: Remove rust and water marks with a commercial stainless steel cleaner, using it as directed. Remove mineral deposits by pouring white vinegar on the stain and rubbing with a dry cloth. For general cleaning, rub along the grain with a cloth dampened with warm water and drops of dish soap. Blot dry to prevent water deposits. Apply a commercial stainless steel polish and buff as directed.

Porcelain enamel: Wipe with a cloth sprayed with all-purpose cleaner. Rinse, and wipe down with a clean cloth. *Tip: Remove stains by filling basin with warm water and adding denture-cleaning tablets.*

Acrylic: Fill the sink with hot water and add ½ cup of bleach (test a dot of bleach on the sink in an inconspicuous area first). Let sit for 30 minutes, then drain and rinse the entire sink. When dry, remove any remaining residue with a washcloth moistened with hot water and dish soap. Buff the surface with a lint-free cloth.

APPLIANCES

Refrigerator/Freezer: Empty all contents and unplug the unit (if freezer is manual-defrost, complete the normal defrost procedure beforehand). Wipe down all interior surfaces with a cloth and a solution of two tablespoons baking soda to one quart of water. Wipe dry with a clean cloth. Clean standard exterior surfaces with an appropriate all-purpose cleaner. Clean stainless steel exteriors with a damp cloth and dish soap, rubbing with the grain, then dry; if desired, polish with a stainless steel polish, as directed.

You can save hundreds of dollars in energy costs over the lifetime of the refrigerator—and extend the lifetime appreciably, with a twice-yearly (more often if you have pets) cleaning of the coils. Unplug the refrigerator and pull it out from the wall to access coils on the back of the unit. (Your coils may be located on the front, behind a vent at the bottom of the refrigerator). If the coils are flat, clean them with a brush. If they are angled, blow them clean with canned air or other compressed air source. Carefully clean the fan blades and around the compressor as well.

Oven—conventional: Remove racks and scrub with dish soap and water, using steel wool for stubborn spots. With racks removed, clean oven interior with nonalkaline oven cleaner, as directed.

Oven—Self-cleaning: Remove and clean racks as described above. Run self-cleaning cycle; when oven cools, wipe down the walls and remove ashes with a damp cloth.

Vent hood: Soak the filter for 10 minutes in hot water with dish soap. Wipe down the hood with hot, soapy water; dry with a clean cloth.

Updating Bathrooms

The three key words to keep in mind when fixing up a bathroom are, in order of importance: *clean, new-looking,* and *waterproof.* Nothing turns off house shoppers more quickly than a mildewed, poorly-caulked shower or a visibly worn toilet seat. The room should look as if it hasn't been occupied by anyone except your pathologically fastidious housecleaner.

Replacing fixtures such as tubs, toilets, or showers is necessary only if they have failed or are ugly to the point of distraction. That said, a few inexpensive upgrades can make a big difference in this small but oh-so-important room. If your bathroom has some appealing features, like a clawfoot tub, a vintage sink, or even a window, it makes sense to highlight these focal points and follow their styling when choosing new elements for the space. In all bathrooms, an integrated look should be the primary decorating goal.

This chapter covers all of the mandatory items for your bathroom checklist, including fixtures, sinks, showers and baths, and surfaces. You'll also find lots of tips and tricks for easy upgrades and for making what you have look and work its best. A little money and a lot of elbow grease can beautify almost any bathroom, turning what could be a major liability into a hard-working asset for your home.

Cosmetic Updates

Like cabinet hardware in the kitchen, accessories in the bathroom (towel bars, toilet paper holders, hooks for bathrobes and the like) are little things that do a lot to tie the look of the room together. Replacing them is a quick and easy task with instant payback. Just be sure to take the time to level and secure everything properly, lest you end up with listing hooks, or towel bars that start to pull loose after a couple of weeks.

When shopping for new accessories, choose a style that complements the general decor of the bathroom, as well as the faucets, cabinet hardware, and light fixtures. To eliminate or minimize touch-up work on the walls, measure the trim plates or decorative covers of the existing accessories, and choose new products with plates of the same size or larger. Matching accessories will have the greatest impact toward a unified look.

Whenever possible, anchor accessories into wall studs, for the best holding power. If there's no stud where you need one, use self-tapping drywall anchors to hold the screws. These anchors have a little drill-bit tip that gets the anchor started, and aggressive threads for holding tight to drywall. You drive them in with a drill and standard Phillips-head tip. Go for the metal anchors instead of plastic; the metal are much less likely to break during driving. Self-tapping anchors work with plaster walls, too, but it helps to drill pilot holes for them, to minimize crumbling of the plaster.

Bathroom accessories are usually designed and sold as matching sets that contain towel rods, paper holders, soap dishes, toothbrush holders and more.

Attach mounting hardware for bathroom accessories directly to wall studs wherever you can. Use a stud finder to locate the studs.

Drive self-tapping hollow-wall anchors if you must install mounting hardware where no studs are present. Self-tapping drywall anchors hold much better than cone-shaped anchors, which rely on friction and aren't made to resist pulling forces.

How to Install a Glass Shelf

1 **Position the shelf** where you want it and mark the top centerpoint of each bracket onto the wall.

2 **Make sure the bracket marks** are level, and check for wall studs in the installation area. Either adjust the location of the brackets or install anchors as necessary. Attach the mounting hardware for the brackets.

3 **Fit the brackets** over the mounting hardware and secure with set screws. Add the rod, shelf, or other fitting parts as required.

Small Change, Big Difference

Simply replacing ordinary or worn switch and receptacle coverplates goes a long way toward refreshing a tired bathroom. Coverplates run from a nickel to more than $5, but when upgrading, replace all the coverplates in the bathroom. Look for new plates that bring flair without a lot of irregular surfaces that make them difficult to clean. Brushed metal or bright white plastic plates are good choices for bathrooms because they have a contemporary appearance and suggest a clean, germ-free environment.

Whether your old coverplates are broken or just visually dull, replacing them with new designer plates makes an instant positive impact far beyond the modest expense.

Sinks & Faucets

As in the kitchen, the sink and faucet in a bathroom are major focal points and should be in like-new condition. If your sink is fundamentally sound, a good cleaning should be all it needs (see page 53). If the faucet drips or the handles don't turn smoothly, you'll find replacement parts at your local home center (see info on fixing kitchen faucets on pages 8 and 9). Replace the aerator in the spout if the water flow is uneven (see page 8).

If your old faucet and sink are not worth salvaging, it's a simple job to swap out one or both. Make things easy on yourself by choosing the same style and sink size as the old one. Replacing a faucet means choosing between a standard one-piece (single body) and a two-piece, or widespread, faucet. A two-piece is a little more complicated to install, but the basic process is the same; just follow the manufacturer's directions. Whichever type you choose, check that the faucet will fit the predrilled holes in the sink.

To remove a faucet, turn off shut-off valves near the sink. Disconnect the flexible supply risers from the faucet body tailpieces, using a wrench or pliers. Remove the clevis from the pop-up stopper rod (if any) on the sink and the pivot rod extending from the sink drain. Unscrew the mounting nuts from the faucet tailpieces. A basin wrench will get you into this tight spot, and penetrating oil will help unstick the nuts if they're corroded. Remove the faucet and scrape off any old putty or residue from the sink top with a putty knife, then clean the area thoroughly.

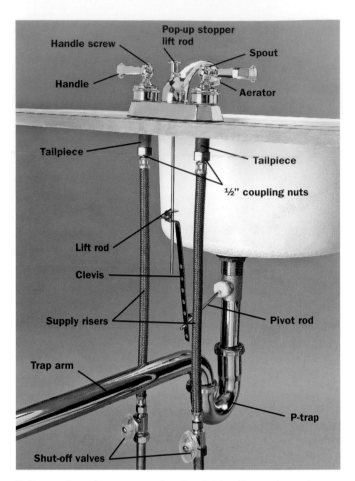

Bathroom faucets are mounted to the sink itself or to the vanity top behind the sink. When replacing a faucet, make sure the supply risers are long enough to reach the new faucet, and buy new braided-steel risers if necessary.

After

Before

Bathroom sinks and faucets are subjected to a constant barrage of grime. They require constant attention and occasional updating. If your old vanity top is ready for retirement, the easiest solution is to find an identical one, or at least one that's the same size and has the same plumbing orientation.

How to Replace a Bathroom Faucet

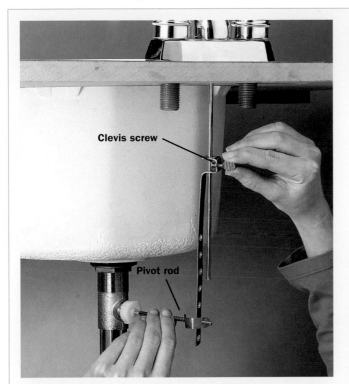

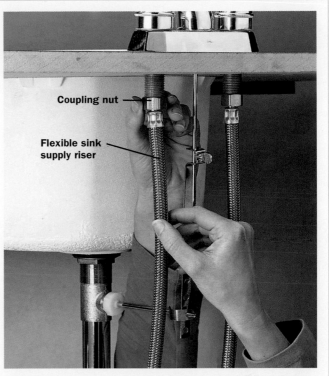

1 **Apply a bead of plumber's putty** around the base of the faucet. Set the faucet in place, and secure the faucet to the sink or vanity top with the supplied washers and mounting nuts. Slide the lift rod of the new faucet into its hole behind the spout. Thread it into the clevis past the clevis screw. Push the pivot rod all the way down, so the stopper is open. With the rod all the way down, tighten the clevis to the lift rod.

2 **Wrap the tailpieces** with Teflon tape and attach the flexible risers. Wrench tighten a half turn past hand-tight. Remove the aerator and turn on the water supplies to flush any debris. Replace the aerator when the water runs clear.

Replacing Bathroom Sinks

To replace a drop-in sink, disconnect the faucet as described on page 36, but leave the faucet attached to the sink. Remove the P-trap by loosening the slip nuts at both ends of the trap; set a bucket underneath to capture the water inside the trap. Plug the drainpipe coming out of the wall with a rag or wadded-up plastic bag.

Cut the caulk joint between sink and vanity top using a utility knife and being careful not to mar the vanity top. Lift out the sink, then clean up any caulk or plumber's putty along the edge of the cutout in the top. Remove the drain flange and tailpiece (it's held in place by a nut on the underside of the sink) from the sink's drain hole. It's a good idea to buy a new drain flange if the old one is stained or the finish is worn.

Install the new faucet (or swap the old one) onto the new sink, following the steps shown on this page. Install the drain flange and tailpiece, adding a bead of plumber's putty under the rim of the drain flange. Assemble the pop-up stopper assembly now, if it's convenient to do so.

Apply a ring of plumber's putty along the edge of the vanity cutout. Set the new sink in place, and make sure it's positioned properly. Press the sink rim down into the putty for a good seal. Hook up the P-trap and faucet connections. Remove any excess putty around the sink rim, then caulk along the vanity top with a thin bead of clear silicone caulk.

Vanity Thrift

If you can find one to fit your vanity, a one-piece vanity top (sink and top molded as one) can save you a pretty penny. You'll find bright white one-piece tops with molded-in backsplash for less than $100, a bargain for such a clean, high-impact bathroom upgrade. That's roughly half the cost of what a separate top-mount or undermount sink and vanity top will set you back (not to mention the extra fuss of installing the sink!).

Toilets

oilets are made of vitreous china, a material that, barring accidental collisions with heavy objects, will easily outlast your house. It's necessary to replace a toilet base (bowl), tank, or tank lid only if it's cracked. You may be able to find a new tank or lid without having to replace the whole works. If the tank leaks but isn't cracked, check the rubber washers at these locations: under the bolts securing the tank to the base; where the flush valve connects to the bottom of the tank; where the ballcock (fill mechanism) meets the tank bottom; and, finally, the large washer between the underside of the tank and the base

(called a spud washer). Replacement parts for all of these are available at home and hardware stores.

If you've ever noticed even slight or intermittent leaking of water between the base and the floor, replace the wax ring that seals the base to the drain opening. You have to remove the toilet to do this, but it's a cheap—and necessary—repair. When you pull the toilet, make sure the subfloor around the drain hasn't become soft and spongy due to water intrusion. *Note: If you remove a toilet base for any reason (such as installing new flooring), you have to replace the wax ring.*

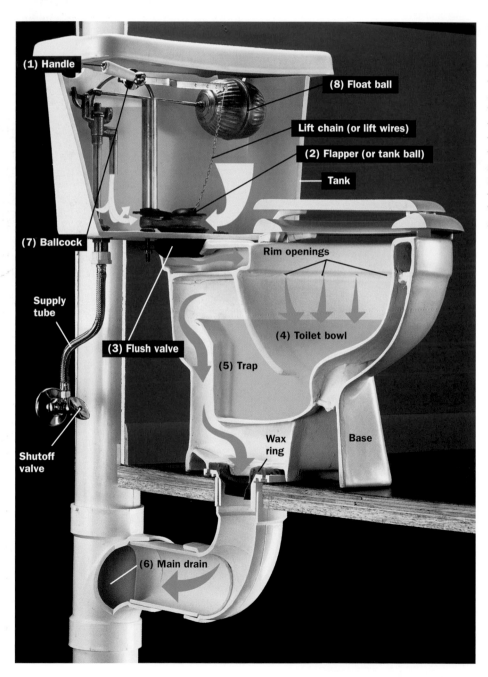

(1) Handle
(8) Float ball
Lift chain (or lift wires)
(2) Flapper (or tank ball)
Tank
(7) Ballcock
Rim openings
Supply tube
(3) Flush valve
(4) Toilet bowl
(5) Trap
Wax ring
Base
Shutoff valve
(6) Main drain

How a toilet works: When the handle (1) is pushed, the lift chain raises a rubber seal, called a flapper or tank ball (2). Water in the tank rushes down through the flush valve opening (3) in the bottom of the tank and into the toilet bowl (4). Waste water in the bowl is forced through the trap (5) into the main drain (6). When the toilet tank is empty, the flapper seals the tank, and a water supply valve, called a ballcock (7), refills the toilet tank. The ballcock is controlled by a float ball (8) that rides on the surface of the water. When the tank is full, the float ball automatically shuts off the ballcock.

Sprucing Up a Toilet

In addition to a thorough cleaning, nothing spruces up an old toilet like a new seat and flush handle. Also buy new decorative bolt caps if they're missing. You can buy a good seat for well under $30. If you're a seller, a basic white plastic seat will show the best—and be sure to buy the right seat for your bowl shape, oval or round.

To replace a toilet seat, pry off the cap covering each of the two bolts at the back of the seat. Remove the bolts with a screwdriver and pliers. Discard the seat, but save the bolts in case you need them for the new seat (you can also buy replacement bolts if the seat doesn't include them). The new seat should go on just like the old one.

Replacing a toilet handle is just as easy as a seat: Lift off the tank lid and locate the chain connecting the handle lever to the round, rubber flapper at the bottom of the tank. Unhook the chain from the lever. Remove the handle nut on the inside of the tank. Technically, this nut is threaded backwards; when viewing from the handle side, turn the nut counterclockwise to loosen it. Pull the handle and lever out through the hole in the tank wall. Install the new handle by reversing this procedure, then check the adjustment on the lever chain.

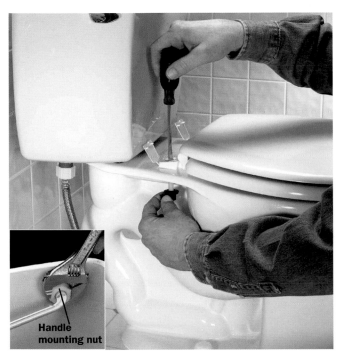

Handle mounting nut

Unbolt the old toilet seat at its hinge mounts, and swap it out with a new seat. Replace a worn handle with a clean, decorative handle by loosening the mounting nuts (inset) that secure the handle inside the tank.

Low-Cost Low-Flow

Modern low-flow toilets are great for saving money on the water bill, but the initial investment—from $125 for a bare-bones basic unit, to over $1,000 for thrones with all the bells and whistles—might give you pause to update. Never fear; you can have the benefits of a low-flow toilet without swapping out your old toilet by using one of a couple of low-tech solutions. Controllable flush handles run $25 to $40 and are simple to install. These allow you to use far less water when a big flush isn't necessary. Or, for a virtually free alternative, add bricks or a bucket full of wet sand to your cistern (toilet tank). These will reduce the amount of water it takes to fill the tank, subsequently reducing the amount of water used in each flush.

Stop That Running Toilet

If your toilet never quite stops filling up after a flush, it's probably due to a faulty ballcock, also known as a fill valve. A new ballcock with a slide-type float (as opposed to the old style with the big float ball tethered to a metal rod) costs less than $10 and is easy to install. Just follow the directions on the product packaging.

Simply insert the threaded end of the valve through the tank hole and secure with the accompanying nut and rubber washer. Attach the cold water supply to the valve (inset).

Troubleshooting Toilet Problems

Problems	Repairs
Toilet handle sticks or is hard to push.	1. Adjust lift wires. 2. Clean and adjust handle.
Handle must be held down for entire flush.	1. Adjust handle. 2. Shorten lift chain or wires. 3. Replace waterlogged flapper.
Handle is loose.	1. Adjust handle. 2. Reattach lift chain or lift wires to lever.
Toilet will not flush at all.	1. Make sure water is turned on. 2. Adjust lift chain or lift wires.
Toilet does not flush completely.	1. Adjust lift chain. 2. Adjust water level in tank. 3. Increase pressure on pressure-assisted toilet.
Toilet overflows or flushes sluggishly.	1. Clear clogged toilet. 2. Clear clogged main waste-vent stack.
Toilet runs continuously.	1. Adjust lift wires or lift chain. 2. Replace leaky float ball. 3. Adjust water level in tank. 4. Adjust and clean flush valve. 5. Replace flush valve. 6. Repair or replace ballcock. 7. Service pressure-assist valve.
Water on floor around toilet.	1. Tighten tank bolts and water connections. 2. Insulate tank to prevent condensation. 3. Replace wax ring. 4. Replace cracked tank or bowl.
Toilet noisy when filling.	1. Open shutoff valve completely. 2. Replace ballcock and float valve. 3. Refill tube is disconnected.
Weak flush.	1. Clean clogged rim openings. 2. Replace old low-flow toilet.
Toilet rocks.	1. Replace wax ring and bolts. 2. Replace toilet flange.

More Quick Fixes for Toilets

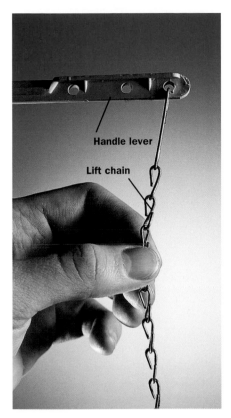

Handle lever

Lift chain

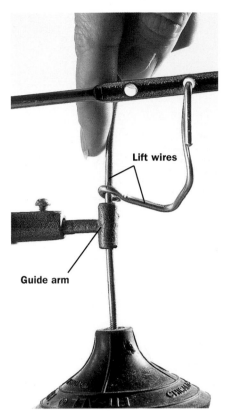

Lift wires

Guide arm

Adjust lift chain so it hangs straight from handle lever, with about ½" of slack. Remove excess slack in chain by hooking the chain in a different hole in the handle lever or by removing links with needlenose pliers. A broken lift chain must be replaced.

Adjust lift wires (found on toilets without lift chains) so that wires are straight and operate smoothly when handle is pushed. A sticky handle often can be fixed by straightening bent lift wires.

On cup-style fill valves, adjust the water level in the tank by shortening or increasing the distance between the float cup and the control lever. Move the spring clip on the cup up down on the pull rod to make the adjustment.

Adjust diaphragm-style fill valves by tightening or loosening the adjustment screw at the top of the valve. This controls the water level in the tank. Lower the water level if it is higher than the top of the overflow tube, and raise it if the flush is weak.

Tank fills too slowly? The first place to check is the shutoff valve where the supply tube for the toilet is connected. Make sure it is fully open. If it is, you may need to replace the shutoff—these fittings are fairly cheap and frequently fail to open fully.

Showers & Tubs

As a rule, expect to have your bathing area carefully inspected by house hunters and guests. First replace all of the old caulking along the tub or shower edges, at the floor, and anywhere seams are formed between surfaces. Don't try to add a new layer of caulk over the old. This just makes a mess and may hide areas where the old caulk is failing without providing an adequate water seal.

If your tub or shower walls are tiled, inspect the grout lines for signs of deterioration. Even the tiniest cracks or holes in grout can let water through, leading to major problems in the underlying wall surface and, potentially, the wall and floor structures. Cracked tiles also permit water intrusion and must be replaced. Caulking the cracks can help for a while, but this looks terrible and won't seal out water for long. If the grout is generally in poor condition but the tiles still look good and are well adhered, you can scrape out the old grout and add new.

If your tub or shower wall grout joints are less than perfect, arm yourself with a strong cleaner, such as oxygen bleach, and a stiff, nylon grout brush to rehab them. Once the grout and tiles are clean, seal the joints with a good grout sealer to help prevent stains.

Just about any tub or shower can benefit from a thorough cleaning and re-caulking of its seams.

How to Replace Caulk

1 **A 5-in-1 tool** works better than a putty or utility knife for removing caulk. Use the tool's razor-sharp tooth to slice caulk from crevices.

2 **Scrub the area** with denatured alcohol to remove grime and film.

3 **Filling—but not overfilling—**the joint is the key to a neat caulk job. Smooth the freshly applied caulk with a damp finger, using a very light touch.

Renewing & Updating Old Tubs

The recommended solutions for fixing up an old tub depend largely upon the type of tub you have. If it's a classic, enameled cast iron clawfoot tub, it's probably worth salvaging and spending some time and money to restore its original beauty. The one major drawback of these traditional gems is that they often lack shower facilities. However, you can update an old tub by adding a shower fixture and curtain rod with a minimum of fuss (see pages 44 to 45).

As for the finish on an old cast iron tub, the only way to restore badly worn or chipped enamel is to have it professionally resurfaced. It's expensive, but the tub will look like new. Be careful shopping for a reglazer and check references. For a cheaper and less comprehensive fix, you can spot repair small chips and cracks with an bathtub repair kit. The results are likely to be less–than perfect, but at least they will decrease the chance that the damage will spread.

Standard enameled steel tubs are nearly as durable as cast iron tubs, but few are valuable enough to warrant resurfacing. Making spot repairs with a repair kit is the answer for chips and other minor surface flaws. If the tub is in poor condition, replace it with a new tub of the same size.

Finally, if your tub is acrylic or fiberglass, you can remove scratches, burn marks, and other surface flaws by sanding them out with ultra-fine sandpaper or emery paper. Sand the affected area using a little bit of water as a lubricant, being careful to remove only what is necessary. Most acrylic tubs are made with color-through material; sanding may dull the finish, but it shouldn't change the color of the surface. You can renew the finish of an acrylic tub, as well as shine up sanded areas, by buffing the surface with an approved polish. Be careful not to polish anti-slip areas of the tub or they'll become dangerously slick when wet.

Perfect Caulk Beads

If you're going to be recaulking more than one bathroom—especially if you're fixing up the bathroom for home buyers, consider buying a powered caulk gun to avoid eyesore caulk seams. Run on batteries, this simple tool helps you lay down a perfect bead of caulk, quickly, easily, and without wasting caulk. Powered caulk guns run around $30.

Repair Kits

Bathtub patch kits can be used for a quick-fix on enameled tub surfaces. These run between $15 and $25 and methods vary kit to kit, so follow the manufacturer's directions precisely. Some kits include tints for blending the finish coat to match your surface. Buy them at hardware stores or home centers.

Plastic, acrylic, and fiberglass tubs and shower surrounds can be buffed and polished effectively with a cleaning-polishing compound and an automotive polisher with a polishing bonnet.

Adding a Shower to a Tub

Complete kits for converting a freestanding tub to a shower are widely available through plumbing supply retailers. A quick online search will give you an idea of what's out there (use key phrases such as clawfoot tub to shower, clawfoot tub shower set, or shower enclosure). Kits include a special faucet with a built-in diverter, a riser pipe (extending from the faucet to the showerhead), and a rectangular shower curtain frame that mounts to the ceiling and wall. Prices range from less than $100 to more than $500, depending on the style of the faucet and showerhead and the quality of the materials.

Examine your faucet and its water hookups carefully before ordering a kit. Measure the distance between the faucet tailpieces and the length and offset of the water supply risers. The new faucet must fit into the existing holes in your tub. You may need to buy new supply risers to connect to the faucet.

To install a shower kit, close the shut-off valves on the water supply lines leading to the old faucet, then disconnect the supply risers from the faucet tailpieces. Then follow the steps on page 45 to complete the job.

A spout with a diverter, some metal supply tubing, and a shower curtain frame can add showering capacity to a standalone tub.

Showerhead Payback

In terms of return on investment, a new showerhead is one of the best home improvement values going—whether you're installing new, as in this project, or replacing an existing one. A basic head with a good spray can cost as little as $10 and a swap-out takes less than five minutes. A top-of-the-line, multi-function, water-saving luxury showerhead can be had for around $50. Low-flow heads save water and money, and this is an upgrade that will be noticed by any house hunter who pulls back the shower curtain—not to mention a treat every time you take a shower.

Replace a showerhead by unscrewing the old head from the shower pipe with channel pliers. Wrap the pipe threads with Teflon tape, then screw on the new head and hand-tighten. Protect the new showerhead by wrapping the jaws of your pliers with tape.

How to Install a Shower Conversion Kit

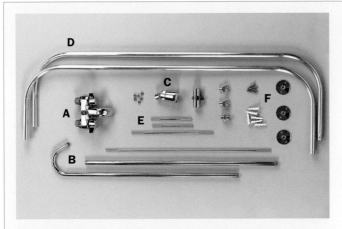

A packaged kit for adding a shower to your tub features a faucet with diverter (A), shower riser plumbing (B), showerhead (C), and a frame for the shower curtain (D) that mounts on the wall and ceiling with threaded rods (E), and fasteners and fittings (F).

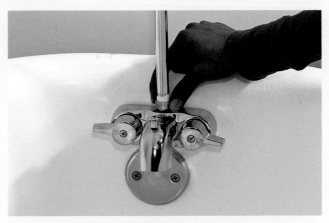

1 **Remove the old tub faucet** and replace it with the new diverter-type faucet from the kit. Fit the assembled shower riser into the top of the faucet and hand-tighten. Apply Teflon tape to the threads before making the connection. This assembly includes one straight and one curved section, joined by a coupling. The top, curved pipe includes a connector to a wall brace. Shorten the straight section using a tubing cutter, to lower the showerhead height, if desired. Slip the compression nut and washer onto the bottom end of the shower riser, and attach the riser to the top of the faucet, hand-tightening for the time being.

2 **With a helper,** assemble the curtain frame, securing with setscrews. Hold the frame level and measure to the ceiling to determine the ceiling brace pipe length. Cut the pipe and complete the ceiling brace assembly. Set the shower riser to the desired height and connect the brace to the wall (ensure strong connections by driving the mounting screws into a wall stud and ceiling joist, if possible.)

3 **After the curtain** frame is completely assembled and secured, tighten the faucet connection with a wrench. Full-size shower kits require one shower curtain on each side of the curtain frame. The hooks seen here feature roller bearings on the tops so they can be operated very smoothly with minimal resistance.

○ Vanities

Standard bathroom vanities and tops are basically small versions of kitchen cabinets and countertops. However, since most people generally have lower expectations when it comes to bathroom materials, you don't have to go out of your way—or your budget—to make the vanity a major showpiece. A fresh paint job on a basic vanity will do the trick (see pages 15 to 17). As for the vanity top, you can renew dulled, stained, or damaged surfaces following the tips given for kitchen countertops (see pages 18 to 23).

This is not to suggest that vanities don't get noticed. They are predominant features in most bathrooms and should be in great condition. If your old vanity isn't worth salvaging or the top is an eyesore, consider replacing the whole shebang. You can buy stock vanities at any large home center from $50 to more than $300, depending on material, size, and accessories. Many are available with a matching top, complete with an integrated sink.

Replacing a Bathroom Vanity

This project shows you how to install a new vanity cabinet and a matching top with integral sink. To prepare for the installation, disconnect the faucet and sink connections, as shown on pages 36 to 37. If you're buying a new faucet for the vanity (usually a good idea), you can install it while the new top is off of the vanity cabinet, following the steps on page 9.

To remove the old vanity cabinet, remove the screws securing the vanity top. Typically, the top is fastened through a mounting bracket at each corner of the cabinet. Cut through any caulk joints between the vanity and the wall, then lift off the top. Next, remove all screws fastening the cabinet to the wall and floor. If you've cut the caulking along the wall, the vanity should lift right out. Scrape off any caulk left on the wall, and clean the floor thoroughly.

Recycled Vanity

If you're upgrading your bathroom, you can save yourself the cost of a new vanity by recycling an old dresser. Many dressers can be easily recycled for service as a vanity. You simply need to find a vanity top that will fit the dresser, or use a dresser that accommodates your current top. Remove the dresser's top and back, and any drawer that impedes the drain and water supplies (attach the drawer front to the frame to maintain the appearance). Otherwise, the dresser is installed as any other vanity (as shown on page 47).

Before

After

Replacing an old vanity cabinet and sink is a cheap and easy upgrade that can shave 10 or 20 years off the appearance of your bathroom.

How to Install a New Vanity

1 **Set the new cabinet in place** so it is centered over the plumbing lines. With the cabinet tight against the wall, check it for level. Shim between the top mounting rail and the wall (at stud locations) as well as underneath the bottom edges of the cabinet to get the vanity cabinet level and plumb. If the fit leaves gaps, you can hide the gaps with trim after the cabinet is installed.

2 **Secure the cabinet to the wall** by driving 3" drywall screws through the back mounting rails and into the wall studs. Drive screws at both sides of the cabinet, at the top and bottom. Trim all exposed shims with a utility knife or chisel. Prepare the vanity top by installing the faucet. Also install the drain tailpiece and flange in the hole of the sink basin (see pages 36 to 37).

3 **Lay a bead of silicone caulk** along the top edge of the vanity and set the vanity top in place. Measure carefully to make sure it's centered. Check the fit of the backsplash against the back wall. If there are any gaps wider than ⅛", scribe the top edge of the backsplash and sand the edge to fit the contours of the wall (follow the manufacturer's directions). Connect the top to the vanity using the fasteners provided with the cabinet.

4 **Assemble the drain parts** and make sure everything is properly aligned. Connect the water supply risers to the faucet, and hook up the pop-up stopper assembly and drain. Apply a fine bead of silicone caulk (use clear or a color that matches the vanity top) where the vanity top meets the wall. For appearance and cleanliness, also caulk where the side edges of the cabinet meet the wall, or add trim to hide wide gaps. Use only as much caulk as is needed, to prevent a messy job.

Flooring

Given their environment, bathroom floors often rank highly on the must-do checklist for home fix-ups. Of course, cleaning is the essential first step. Once that's done, inspect the floor carefully for any areas that may be letting water through to the subflooring. Cracks in tiles and grout, and tears in vinyl flooring, are common culprits.

Old ceramic tile that is still solid underfoot can be renewed with dramatic results. Start by scrubbing the grout joints with a strong cleaner, such as oxygen bleach (page 22) or a commercial grout-and-tile cleaner. For more severe problems, like deteriorated or badly stained grout or broken tiles, make the repairs described on the following pages.

With sheet vinyl flooring, you may be able to patch damaged areas (see pages 24 to 25), or consider replacing the flooring. Bathroom floors are usually small enough to be covered with a single piece of sheet vinyl. The basic process of installing new sheet vinyl is described on pages 26 to 27.

Vinyl tiles can be cleaned up and damaged tiles can be replaced (see page 25), although a better option may be to cover the old floor with new sheet vinyl.

Choosing new bathroom flooring is pretty straightforward. It should be waterproof and fairly slip-resistant, so you don't have to worry about wiping up every drop of water to prevent an accident. You can quickly narrow down the options to ceramic (or porcelain) or glass tile, and sheet vinyl, or linoleum. In a small half-bath or powder room, you can get away with vinyl tiles, wood, or laminate, but any room with a tub or shower needs a seamless water barrier, period. And carpet doesn't belong on a bathroom floor.

Thrifty Tile Floors

You can save money on a ceramic tile bathroom floor by using 12-inch- or 16-inch-square tiles, rather than smaller 4-inch or 6-inch tiles of the same material. The larger tiles will cost less per square foot, are easier and quicker to lay out and install, and look more natural on a floor.

Failed grout allows water underneath tiles, which causes damage to spread rapidly. If the grout lines in your tile floor are crumbling or a few tiles are a loosened, the best solution is to regrout the entire floor.

Inspecting & Cleaning Floors

To determine if your grout needs to be resealed, test the existing sealer by putting a few drops of water on a grout line. If the water beads up, the sealer is still working. If the water absorbs into the grout, it needs to be resealed.

Remove tough stains with mineral spirits or household bleach. Wet a rag with the solution, and place it over the stain. Lay a plastic bag over the rag to slow evaporation. Wait 1 to 2 hours, then wipe up the stain. Always test solvents in an inconspicuous area before using them elsewhere on the floor. Bleach may strip the protective finish off the floor, leaving it dull. If this happens, refinish.

On vinyl and laminate, you can remove tough spots like shoe polish or tar with nail polish remover containing acetone. When the spot is gone, wipe the area with a clean, damp cloth.

For heavy stains on natural stone tile, try a manufacturer poultice specifically for porous stone materials. Cover the stain with the poultice, then tape plastic over it. Let the poultice set, according to the manufacturer's instructions, then remove it.

Regrouting Tile

The process of removing old grout and filling the cleaned joints with new grout is the same for most ceramic, porcelain, stone, and glass tile installations (including floors, walls, and countertops). Grout is a masonry material made with Portland cement, pigment, and additives. Grout for floor tile usually includes sand, which adds strength to the larger grout joints in floor installations. As a general rule, use plain (non-sanded) grout for joints up to 1/16-inch wide, and use sanded grout for joints wider than 1/16 inch. Grout is sold in premixed, dry-powder form for about $15 a bag, or liquid form for about twice that, in a wide range of colors. Mix the powder for application according to the product directions, so the consistency is roughly that of toothpaste. For improved adhesion and waterproofing, use a polymer-modified grout mix.

It's important to note that regrouting is an appropriate repair only for tile that is securely bonded to its substrate. Several loose tiles in an area indicate that the adhesive has failed, or there are problems (usually moisture related) with the substrate. If multiple tiles are loose, re-tiling the floor may be your only option. It is best to replace all of the grout within an area.

To remove old grout, start scraping out the joints with a grout saw. Try to remove all of the grout from the tile edges. If small sections are really stubborn, it's acceptable to leave them in place and grout over them, because they're not likely to come loose.

With the grout removed, vacuum the joints thoroughly, and clean the tile and joints with a cleaner recommended by your tile supplier. Rinse well and let the area dry. Mix as much grout as you can apply in about 15 minutes. It sets in about 30 minutes, and you'll need time to sponge the joints before the grout sets.

Drop the mixed batch of grout onto the tile (for walls, apply the grout with your grout float). Holding a grout float at 30 degrees to the surface, spread the grout over the tiles and joints, forcing it into the joints and filling them completely.

When the joints are filled, make another pass with the float held almost perpendicular to the surface to remove excess grout from the joints and tile; move the float diagonally to the joints, to prevent pulling grout from the joints.

After about 15 minutes from the initial mixing, swipe across the joints diagonally, using a damp—not wet—grout sponge. Rinse the sponge frequently as you work. If the grout is pulling out of the joints, either the grout hasn't set up enough or you're wiping too hard. When you're done, the grout joints should be smooth and level, and the tile faces should be free of grout, with only a light residue left behind.

Repeat and, 15 minutes after each section is sponged, wipe the grout residue from the tile with a clean, dry rag). Make sure all of the tile faces are clean before letting the grout cure for 72 hours, or as directed. Finish by applying a recommended sealer to the grout joints.

Sanded grout is a dry powder that's sold in bags and then mixed with water for grouting tile joints that are wider than 1/16".

Glass Tile Grout

Glass tile continues to gain in popularity for use as flooring and countertops in the bathroom and the kitchen. But if you choose this intriguing and beautiful alternative to ceramic tile, save yourself money, time, and effort by using a flexible urethane grout with the tiles. Glass expands and contracts more than ceramic does, which means traditional mixed grout will break down much quicker when used with glass tiles. Urethane grout is about three times as expensive as standard powdered grout, but is easier to use and will make up for the additional expense in longevity.

Carbide-blade grout saws are used to remove failing grout.

How to Regrout Tile

1 **Scrape out the old grout** with a grout saw or other tool, being careful not to scratch the tile faces or chip the edges. You can re-grout only the filed grout lines for a quick fix, but for more pleasing results and to prevent color variation in the grout, remove the grout around all tiles and re-grout the entire floor.

2 **Wash the tiled floor** with a 1-to-1 mix of white vinegar and water, paying special attention to the areas around the tile joints. Vacuum the floor first to get rid of all debris.

3 **Apply new grout.** Prepare sanded grout mix according to the instructions on the package and then pack fresh grout deep into the joints, using a rubber grout float. Hold the float at a 30-degree angle to the tiled surface.

4 **Wipe diagonally across the tiles** and grouted joints to remove excess grout and smooth the joints. Seal the grout joints with grout sealer after they've dried for a week or so. *Note: Sealing all the grout joints will help new grout lines blend with old grout if you're only doing a partial re-grouting.*

Lights & Mirrors

The right lighting and an attractive, functional mirror can make a bathroom look great and more pleasant to use. A sink and vanity area calls for task-level lighting, yet many are illuminated by a strip fixture above the mirror, or worse, by recessed lights in the ceiling. These do a great job of illuminating the top of your head, while your face remains in the shadows. The best way to brighten a vanity area is with wall fixtures mounted at head-level on both sides. Side lights cast even light across your face, which is, for better or worse, what you're usually trying to see in detail when you're at work in front of the mirror.

Lighting designers recommend that vanity fixtures deliver a combined output of at least 150 watts for standard lightbulbs, or the equivalent wattage with fluorescent lamps. If, for practical reasons, a fixture must go above the vanity mirror, it should be at least 24 inches long and hang at a height of 75 to 80 inches above the floor.

Bathroom mirrors come in an endless range of sizes and styles, so you can easily find something that fits your room and budget. Frameless mirrors mount flush to the wall with simple corner clips (large mirrors usually require a metal channel along the bottom). You can buy them cut-to-fit from any glass and mirror supplier, and at some home centers. Framed mirrors hang on the wall just like any picture frame.

Design principles dictate that a vanity mirror should be no wider than the vanity itself. If side light fixtures are included, they can extend a little beyond the sides of the vanity, but the mirror-and-light composition should fit the proportions of the vanity unit and the supporting wall.

To upgrade the illumination in your bathroom with vanity mirror sidelights, start by turning off power at the service panel and removing the old fixtures. Remove wall surfaces from around the mirror so that you can access the existing junction box. Mark the locations of the fixtures and install new electrical boxes. If the location is on or next to a stud, you can attach the box directly to the stud. Otherwise, you'll need to install blocking or use adjustable braces.

The rest of the process is a matter of straightforward wiring. If you're unsure of your electrical skills, hire an electrician to connect the lights.

How to Install a Tilting Wall Mirror

1 **Determine the height of the mirror mounts** by dividing the overall height of the mirror by two and adding the result to the number of inches above the vanity you want the bottom edge of the mirror to be placed. In this case, the mirror came with a mounting template. Tape the template to the wall and drill two 5/16" holes at each of the mounting post locations.

2 **Insert the included wall anchors** and tap into place. Remove the brackets from the mounting posts by loosening the setscrew. Attach the brackets to the wall at the wall anchor locations.

3 **Assemble the mirror if necessary.** Make sure the setscrews on the mounting posts are facing downward. Carefully lift the mirror, place the mounting posts over the brackets, and slide into place. Tighten the setscrews.

Money in Motion

A guest bathroom or seldom-used master bathroom is the perfect candidate for the money and energy savings offered by a motion-activated light switch. Although these innovative devices run about $25, you will likely make the investment back in energy savings.

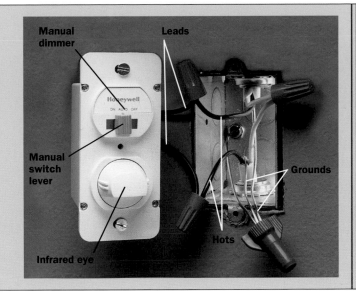

Cleaning Bathroom Surfaces

SINK

Porcelain enamel: Wipe from top to bottom with a cloth sprayed with all-purpose cleaner/disinfectant. Rinse, then dry with a clean cloth. *Tip: Remove stains by filling the basin with warm water and adding denture-cleaning tablets.*

Solid-surface—matte/satin finish: Apply a few drops of dish soap to a damp cloth, then wring out. Wipe the sink from top to bottom in a circular motion. Rinse, then dry with a clean cloth.

Solid-surface—gloss finish: Dunk a cloth in a solution of equal parts water and white vinegar; wring out. Wipe the sink from top to bottom in a circular motion.

Vitreous china: Wipe from top to bottom in a circular motion, using a cloth sprayed with glass cleaner. Rinse, then dry with a clean cloth.

FAUCET

All types: Use a toothbrush, cotton swab, or dental floss to remove mineral deposits and grime from crevices.

Chrome: Wipe surfaces with a cloth and water, or a cloth sprayed with glass cleaner.

Nickel: Buff surfaces with a clean, dry cloth. Wipe again with a cloth sprayed with glass cleaner, and let dry.

Stainless steel: Wipe with a cloth dampened with water and a small amount of dish soap. Dry with a clean cloth. Apply a commercial stainless steel polish as directed.

TUB & SHOWER

Porcelain enameled steel/cast iron: Rub in a circular motion with a damp cloth and dish soap (abrasive pads and cleansers can scratch porcelain). Clean the drain flange with a toothbrush. Rinse. Dry with a clean cloth.

Acrylic/fiberglass: Apply a mild abrasive cleanser (such as Soft Scrub) to the surface. Wait 5 minutes, then rub in a circular motion with a cloth. Rinse. Clean the drain flange with a toothbrush. Dry with a clean cloth.

Glass/fiberglass shower doors: Remove soap scum by rubbing in circles with a brush dipped in white vinegar. *Note: Do not use vinegar on laminated glass. Remove lime deposits by rubbing with a cloth and lemon oil. Finish cleaning with glass cleaner.*

VANITY CABINETS

Cabinet fronts: Clean with a cloth and appropriate cleaner working from top to bottom. Rinse with a clean water-dampened cloth to remove all cleaner residue. Wipe shelves with a slightly dampened cloth (water and dish soap); dry.

VANITY COUNTERTOPS

Laminate: Rub in a circular motion using a moist sponge or soft nylon pad sprayed with all-purpose cleaner (abrasive cleansers and steel wool or stiff brushes can scratch laminate). Rinse with a water-dampened cloth.

TOILET

Inside bowl: Clean with toilet-bowl cleaner or a mild abrasive cleanser and a toilet brush. Flush to rinse.

Clean outer surfaces with a cloth and all-purpose cleaner/disinfectant. Rinse with a clean, wet cloth.

Updating Living Areas

Living and dining rooms, bedrooms, and the hallways can be treated similarly by the fixer-upper because they're all decorated in the same way. In this chapter, we'll cover living spaces from floor to ceiling, along with quick fixes and updates for some of the little things, like switches, thermostats, and smoke alarms.

Ask any number of real estate agents to name the two things you should do to improve a home, and they're bound to say the same thing: "Paint everything and replace the carpet." A fresh coat of paint usually costs less than $50 and has a transformative quality that goes well beyond erasing the scuffs and stains of everyday life. A new shade of paint also rids walls of ugly colors that never quite hit the mark. Replacing carpets is certainly not necessary in every case. Sometimes a good cleaning and a spot repair or two can make a quality carpet look almost new. As for other types of flooring, most can be cleaned, repaired, or renewed to be in harmony with your freshly painted walls.

With the painting and floors done, you can focus your attention on quickie upgrades, such as new switch plates, outlet covers, and heating registers—inexpensive little touches that dress up a room. Finally, we'll show you how an inexpensive organizer can make every inch of bedroom closet space count.

Walls & Ceilings

Because it's always best to patch and paint the ceiling before the walls, we'll tackle ceilings first. By virtue of their location, ceilings tend to receive the least amount of everyday abuse. However, they are usually the first surfaces to show signs of water damage from a leaky roof, and they fight their own private battle with the steady pull of gravity over the years. Like walls, ceilings are also vulnerable to the ravages of ill-conceived decorating fads, as evidenced by the ubiquitous popcorn texture applied to most living room ceilings in '60s and '70s era homes.

Common Ceiling Repairs

The following repairs pertain primarily to drywall ceilings. If you have plaster ceilings, you can hide cracks and minor surface flaws with regular drywall compound, then hand-texture the repair to match the original surface. However, if you detect any sagging in a plaster ceiling—caused by the plaster surface layer pulling away from its supporting framework of lath—leave it alone and call a professional. It's not uncommon for large (and very heavy) sections of plaster to fall from ceilings when disturbed.

Ceiling damage is usually caused by a combination of water and gravity. Water that drips onto a ceiling surface eventually works its way through, leaving telltale stains on the surface. Gravity is especially a problem if builders used ⅜-inch drywall on ceilings, or spaced joists too far apart. In the old days (before drywall screws) most contractors used nails to fasten ceiling panels, which can be a problem because the weight of the panels tugs on the nails, causing them to slip in some instances.

To repair a damaged seam in a ceiling, cut back any loose joint tape to a point where it's still well adhered. Scrape along the exposed seam with a 6-inch drywall knife to smooth the surface and bring it as close as possible to bare drywall. Also scrape off any texture for 6 inches on both sides of the seam. Make sure the panel edges are securely fastened to the framing above. If necessary, drive 1¼-inch coarse-thread drywall screws every few inches along the edges.

Using the 6-inch drywall knife, fill the seam with all-purpose drywall compound, then add a 3-inch-wide, ⅛-inch-thick layer of compound centered over the seam. Embed a strip of paper joint tape into the compound, and smooth it out with the knife, pressing firmly to flatten the tape and squeeze out most of the compound from behind it. Let the joint dry overnight. Add one or two finish coats, then texture the surface to blend in the repair. Seal water-stained drywall with a primer/sealer (see page 65).

A popcorn ceiling is no treat if you are trying to sell a house (or just keep it clean, for that matter). The best thing about textured ceiling treatments is that they are easy to remove.

Premixed joint compound (right) is convenient, but it tends to shrink and crack and the shelf-life isn't very long once the tub is opened. Dry bagged joint compound (left) can be mixed with water in small batches, dries smoothly, and comes in a wider range of types with special application and drying characteristics.

Repairing Sagging Ceilings

Common signs of a sagging ceiling are cracks along the edges near the walls and a wavy ceiling surface. You can also tell that a panel is sagging by pushing up on the panel where it's fastened to a joist: The panel will yield somewhat, and you may see nail heads pop out slightly. The quick fix for this is quite simple. First, use a studfinder to locate the ceiling joists. At each joist, push up the panel tight against the joist and drive a 1¼-inch coarse-thread drywall screw about every 6 inches along the joist. Drive the screws slightly deeper than flush without breaking through the drywall's face paper.

The old fasteners will probably begin popping out as you refasten the panel. Wherever this happens, drive a screw about 2 inches from each popout, then hammer the old nail back in, leaving a slight dimple in the surface. When all sagging areas are refastened, cover the screw heads and nail heads with joint compound, using a four-inch drywall knife or a putty knife. Add a second coat of compound after the first coat dries. Sand the final coat smooth, if necessary.

Saving Future Repair Costs

A ceiling stain or water-damaged section is usually a sign of water leak—most often through the roof or siding. It can also be the first sign of a water problem. Water can wick over great distances, so it's important to determine exactly where the leak comes from by following the trail (it should be fairly obvious and will run along ceiling joists to the point where the water drips down from the leak). Remedy the leak before fixing the ceiling, and you'll save yourself major water damage repairs down the road.

A roof leak inevitably leaves a trail. Follow it to the source and remedy to save bigger repair costs in the future.

● How to Repair a Sagging Drywall Ceiling

1 **Position a T-brace** under the lowest point of the sagging area with the bottom end on a piece of plywood or hardboard on the floor. Nudge it forward until the sagging panels are tight to the joists. If fasteners pop through the surface, drive them back in.

2 **Remove loose tape and compound** at joints between loose panels. Starting at one end, drive wallboard screws with broad, thin washers every 4" through the center of the joint and into the joists. In the field of panel, drive screws 2" from existing fasteners.

3 **When the area is securely fastened,** remove the T-brace. Scrape off any loose chips of paint or wallboard around joints and screws, then fill with compound. Cover large cracks or gaps with fiberglass tape before applying the compound.

Dealing with Popcorn Ceiling Texture

The first step in dealing with a popcorn ceiling texture is to remove a sample and send it in to a local lab to have it tested for asbestos. A lot of pre-1980 homes have popcorn ceilings made with the cancer-causing material. The last thing you want to do is start scraping and sanding it off, spreading the fibers throughout your home and HVAC system. To find a lab, look in the phone book under Asbestos/Environmental Testing and Consulting. You can have a sample tested within a day or two for about $45. Ask the lab for recommendations on safe removal and storage of the sample, and/or refer to the U.S. EPA's website (www.epa.gov) for more information.

If the lab results show no asbestos, proceed to the next step: removing the texture. If the sample tests positive for asbestos, inquire at your local waste disposal agency. In some areas you'll be required to hire an abatement contactor to remove the material, but in others you may be allowed to do it yourself if you follow the very exacting removal and disposal guidelines.

To remove asbestos-free popcorn ceiling texture, first cover the floors and walls with plastic sheeting, taped together at the seams. Then lay down sheets of cardboard to create a non-slip surface. Follow the steps below and, when all of the texture is gone, let the ceiling dry completely. Fill in holes, nail pops or gouges with joint compound, and let dry overnight. Sand the dry compound with a 150-grit sanding sponge to smooth out imperfections.

If the ceiling is smooth enough, begin priming and painting. A stippled paint job with a heavy-nap roller or texture paint can help hide imperfections. If, however, the surface flaws are clearly noticeable, it probably needs a skim coat of drywall compound. This is skilled work, so you should consider hiring a pro for the skim coat, or give yourself plenty of time for practicing first.

No-Fuss Test Kits

Home asbestos test kits are widely available in home centers and hardware stores. Most exceed EPA testing standards and offer a quick and easy way to test for asbestos. The kits usually cost about $30 and come with simple, easy-to-use instructions.

Cleaning Textured & Acoustical Ceilings

Heavy ceiling textures and acoustical ceiling tiles can be difficult, if not impossible, to clean. There are pros who can help. Look in the phone book under Ceiling Cleaners or Ceiling Contractors, and inquire about a "touchless" cleaning process. This involves spraying a non-toxic chemical solution onto the ceiling surface and letting it dissolve the fatty film that traps dust, grease, smoke particles, and other forms of crud. The ugly stuff simply vanishes, and no rinsing is needed.

How to Remove Ceiling Texture

Fill a hand-pump sprayer with a solution of one teaspoon dish soap to one gallon of water. Spray the ceiling and wait about 20 minutes, then test the texture by scraping with a 6" drywall knife. If it's too dry, make a second pass with the sprayer. However, try not to saturate the face paper of the underlying drywall, which makes it vulnerable to tears.

Once saturated, scrape off the texture with a 6" drywall knife. Don't let the photo fool you; this is a very messy job. Scrape the entire surface systematically with the knife. Work carefully, leaving the surface smooth without damaging the drywall paper

Patching Damaged Walls

Most homes end up with a few holes or cracks here and there, whether from doorknobs impaling the wall, improperly hung pictures, or basic settling of the structure. Small holes and cracks—no bigger than a dime—can be filled with spackle or drywall compound, then smoothed over with a couple more coats of compound. The finish coats are needed because the initial fill-coat will shrink quite a bit, leaving a shallow depression in the surface.

To repair doorknob-size holes, cover the hole with two strips of self-adhesive mesh drywall tape. Coat the area with a thin layer of drywall mud, pressing a little extra compound into the tape where the hole is. Let the mud dry overnight, then add one or more thin finish coats to hide the tape and feather the repair into the surrounding wall surface. Sand and prime the area before painting. *Tip: You can use this same repair for small holes in plaster walls. Or, if the hole is shallow, you can skip the tape and fill the hole with plaster repair compound or a few layers of drywall mud. Patching large holes in drywall requires a little more work, as described on* *page 61.*

Cutting Drywall Repair Costs

Buying all the loose elements to repair a drywall crack or hole often means purchasing far more materials than you'll need or use. Even a modest pail of spackle, a roll of mesh tape, and a package of sandpaper will accommodate more wall defects than you're likely to deal with in the life of your home. For a cheaper, handier alternative, investigate drywall repair kits. These all-in-one packages provide everything you'll need—compound, mesh tape, sanding blocks or paper—plus extras such as screws to secure patches, special clips for stabilizing cracks, and complete instructions to help you get achieve a perfectly smooth wall with a minimum of effort. Drywall kits range in price from $7 to $15, depending on the size and complexity of the repair they're meant for.

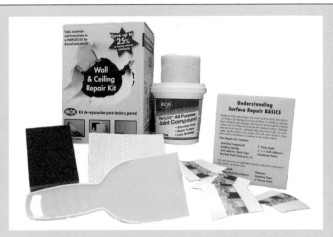

A drywall repair kit makes fixing a hole or crack easier and quicker.

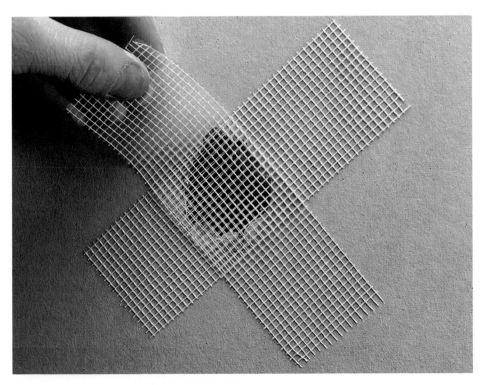

Patch smallish holes with crossed strips of mesh drywall tape and three coats of drywall compound. The tape strengthens the repair and minimizes compound shrinkage and cracking.

How to Repair Cracks in Walls

1 **Prepare cracks in drywall** by cutting a V-shaped groove along the crack, using a utility knife. Try to make the sides of the groove as clean as possible.

Variation: For cracks in plaster walls, undercut the crack with a utility knife or a "church key" bottle opener. Clear out all the loose debris, widening the crack as necessary to remove unstable plaster.

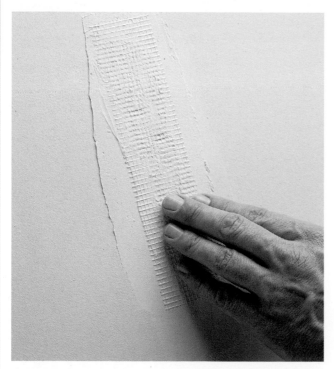

2 **Fill the crack** completely by forcing compound into it with a four-inch drywall knife or broad putty knife. Set a strip of mesh tape into the compound, centered over the crack. Apply a layer of compound over the tape and let it dry.

3 **Apply additional layers** of compound over the tape. It may take up to three layers to completely conceal the tape. Sand the final coat lightly until smooth, and feather the edges into the surrounding wall surface.

How to Repair a Hole in the Wall

1 **Mark cutout lines** around the damaged area. The shape of the cutout isn't important, but square lines make it easier to cut the patch material.

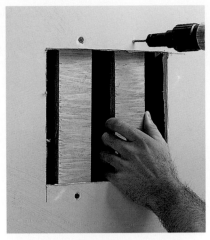

2 **Insert backing strips** of scrap lumber into the wall behind the damaged area and attach the strips with drywall screws driven through the wall around the perimeter of the repair area.

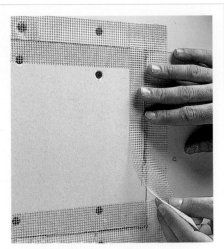

3 **Finish the joints** around the patch with self-adhesive drywall joint tape and apply and sand joint compound.

Finishing Wall & Ceiling Repairs

The secret to making a patch or repair job blend in is to use multiple thin finish coats of joint compound to conceal the repair. Then texture the repair area to match the existing surface treatment. For untextured walls and ceilings, the trick lies in adding progressively broader (but thinner) finish coats for a smooth transition to the original surface.

Apply the first coat of joint compound with a six-inch drywall knife, filling the seams and applying just enough on top to fill the holes in the mesh tape (with paper tape, the first coat doesn't need to cover the top of the paper). After the compound dries, sand it smooth with a 150-grit sanding sponge.

Apply the second coat over the entire area, using a 10- or 12-inch drywall knife (a six-inch knife is okay for small repairs). Feather the compound flush with the surrounding surface. Let the second coat dry, then sand it smooth. At this point, you shouldn't see any of the drywall tape. If necessary, apply a third coat of compound. Let the compound dry, then sand.

Texturing a patch may require some trial and error, but if at first you don't succeed, scrape off the texture while it's still wet and try again. You can mimic most drywall and plaster textures with standard drywall compound, using your hand or any tool that will do the trick. Just lay on some joint compound to an appropriate thickness, then work it to approximate the original texture. Alternatively, you can use spray texture to reproduce popcorn textures or professionally applied effects. Be warned, however, that canned ceiling texture is very difficult to work with.

Canned spray-on ceiling texture can cover up small-area repairs, but the product is very tricky to control.

An Easy Textured Ceiling Solution

Stripping a textured ceiling can be a messy, unpleasant task, as can texturing a repair. Sometimes the easier solution is to just cover the ceiling with ¼" drywall. This is also a potentially much cheaper alternative to abating asbestos-laden popcorn ceilings. Many codes allow for capping asbestos texturing with a layer of drywall. The drywall should be securely attached with construction adhesive and drywall screws, screwed into the ceiling joists. Check with your local building department to determine if this solution is allowed in your municipality.

Removing Wallpaper

Wallpaper tends to generate strong opinions. That's why real estate professionals recommend against hanging wallpaper (or even keeping old paper) before putting a house on the market. If you've just bought a fixer-upper, chances are good that you've already made plans to tear off some dated or worn wallpaper left by the previous owners.

Fortunately, most wallpaper sold in recent decades is made to be stripped without too much trouble. Standard vinyl papers have a thin, vinyl top layer that protects the paper layers beneath and provides a washable, water-resistant surface. To remove the wallpaper, you have to strip off the vinyl layer, then attack the paper layers with water. Some vinyl papers can be stripped off in one pass.

To start removing old wallpaper, look for a loose edge and, with the help of a wide putty knife, peel up the top layer. If everything comes up at once, great—you've got "strippable" paper. More than likely, however, you'll just be peeling off the protective vinyl layer, along with the decorative layer beneath, leaving a thick layer of paper that's glued to the wall. Be patient, and take the time to remove every last inch of the plastic film.

If the layers of the covering won't separate and you're getting nowhere with the stripping, you may have to abandon this step and go buy a perforating tool (or wallpaper scorer). Run the tool all over the wall to create thousands of tiny holes in the wallpaper. The holes will let water or a chemical stripper penetrate to the adhesive behind the paper.

Prepare for this process by covering the floor and baseboards with plastic and tape.

Of course, if you're a fan of wallpaper or don't have the time to strip an entire wall, you can spruce up any problem areas using the techniques discussed on page 63.

Lastly, if you're dealing with thin wallpaper or an older or specialized type, it may be impossible to remove without seriously damaging the wallboard underneath (wallpaper should always be installed over primed or painted walls for just this reason). In this case, you can leave the paper and paint over it. Simply remove any loose sections, skim coat holes, dings, gouges, or low areas as well as the seams, and sand smooth. Then prime with an oil-based primer, and paint with the topcoat color of your choice.

A wallpaper scorer perforates the waterproof coating so wallpaper stripping solution can penetrate into the glue layer between the wallpaper and the wall.

● How to Remove Wallpaper

1 **Score the wallpaper** all over with a scoring tool to allow moisture to soak the paper. Combine water and stripping solution in a hand-pump sprayer, and spray the wall top to bottom. Let soak and repeat as necessary—often three times. Collect excess fluid with a sponge at the bottom of the wall.

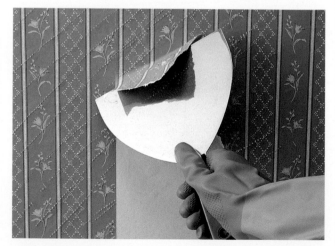

2 **Scrape away saturated paper and adhesive** with a wide putty or putty knife. Use a damp sponge to remove residue and rinse with clean water when done. Allow the wall to dry thoroughly before painting.

How to Repair Wallpaper Damage

PATCHING DAMAGE

1 **To replace a damaged section of wallpaper,** tape a scrap of matching wallpaper over the damaged area. Align so that the patterns match.

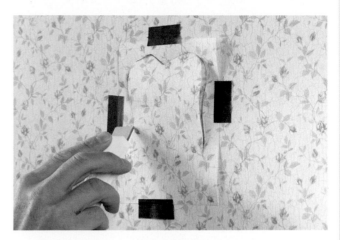

2 **Cut through both layers of wallpaper** with a utility knife equipped with a new blade. Remove the scrap and damaged section, and then apply wallpaper adhesive to the back of the patch and press it in place. Roll patch and wipe clean with a damp sponge.

FIXING BUBBLES

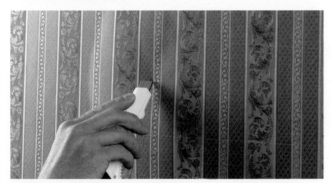

1 **Fix a bubble** by piercing with a sharp utility knife, making a tiny slit. Cut along any line in the pattern of the wallpaper to better hide the slit.

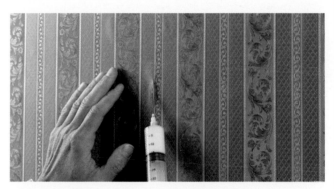

2 **Insert the tip of a glue syringe** through the slit and apply a small amount of wallpaper adhesive. Press the wallpaper down firmly to bond it with the wall or paper underneath. Use a damp sponge to wipe away any excess adhesive.

Inspect the Wall

Thoroughly removing wallpaper takes some work. Often, you may think you've got all of the residue scraped off, only to find there are bumps and flaws once you begin to paint. To inspect the walls after cleaning (and before painting), shine a lamp from the side to highlight imperfections that may not show up under direct or overhead light.

Painting Living Spaces

Painting walls, ceilings, and trim is hands-down the quickest and cheapest way to spruce up your fixer-upper. But before we get into specific techniques and strategies, here's a word of advice: There's no such thing as a "quickie" paint job. It takes nearly as much time to do a bad job as it does to do it right. You still have to clean the walls, tape and cover everything you don't want painted, and put on enough paint to completely hide the old surface. In fact, rushing the project usually takes more time in the long run, because you have to go back and touch up missed spots, and you'll probably have more paint splatters and messes to clean up from the careless work.

Doing the job right begins with the right paint. Bargains in paint often aren't bargains at all. Remodelers on a budget often use the least expensive paint they can find and plan on doing two or more coats. Or they spend more for one-coat paint and hope to cover everything in one go. When it comes down to it, low-quality paints aren't really that much cheaper than good, mid-grade paints (bargain brands start at around $13 while quality name brands start at about $20), and the former almost never cover as well. Also, the colors aren't as true or as rich with low-quality paints, and they tend to fade more quickly than with better paints. The main knock against one-coat paints is that they don't always live up to their primary claim of one-coat coverage.

The one-coat strategy works best when the new paint is darker than the old, for obvious reasons. If you're trying to change a wall from burgundy to antique white, for example, your best bet is to prime the walls with a less-expensive base primer, then use a better-quality paint for the finish coat (or coats). In general, instead of spending extra for a so-called one-coat paint, look for a good-quality, ordinary paint that is rated highly for coverage. Several products that are rated best for coverage are available for around $20 a gallon. When it's time to paint, lay on a consistent, heavy coat and let it dry. If you're satisfied with the coverage, great. If not, apply another light coat of the same paint.

Cost-Effective Primer

Tinted primer—standard primer tinted with a color matching or close to your top coat—can save you the time and effort of a second topcoat. The primer prepares the surface as any standard white primer would, but provides a compatible colored base for the top coat. If you've chosen a standard paint color from the paint company's palette, you can usually match that color in a tinted primer. For darker colors, many paint companies offer primers in shades of grey designed to enhance the top coat. Either way, a tinted primer will set you back about $3 or $4 more per gallon than standard white, but can very well save you the expense and time of an additional top coat.

Lessons from the Pros

- **Plan to paint in the proper order.** Do the ceilings, then the trim, then the walls.
- **Most pros like to "cut in" the edges** of an area first, then roll, brush, or spray the main field. Cut in with a good brush, and lay the paint on thick so you have to do it only once.
- **When painting trim,** or painting surfaces around trim, pros don't normally use masking tape as most amateurs do. They simply freehand the edges with a high-quality brush—usually a sash brush. Tape is undesirable because it takes time to apply, and it often lets paint seep underneath, leaving you with a sloppy line and extra mess to clean up.
- **Trim should be caulked** wherever it meets wall or ceiling surfaces, and the caulk should be overlapped by the wall or ceiling paint.

A fresh coat of paint on the walls and ceiling makes the whole room feel cleaner and, in some cases, larger.

Painting Ceilings

The standard choice of paint for ceilings in living areas is flat white (often pretinted and labeled as Ceiling White). Flat paint hides imperfections better than glossier sheens, and you don't need the washability of satin or eggshell on a ceiling.

If the ceiling is clean and is white or a light color, you probably don't need a primer. Living rooms with wood-burning fireplaces and dining rooms near kitchens may need a thorough cleaning with TSP (trisodium phosphate) to remove soot and cooking residue. Also be sure to seal any water-stained areas with a good primer/sealer.

Cover the floor with a drop cloth, wrap the light fixtures in plastic bags, and get down to painting. First, cut in along the edges of the ceiling with a sash brush, making a three-inch band along the perimeter. If you're painting the walls a similar color to the ceiling, you can save time by letting the paint lap onto the walls slightly while cutting in.

The easiest way to paint a ceiling is with a roller sleeve on an extension pole. For smooth-texture ceilings, use a ⅜"-nap synthetic roller cover. Work in three-foot-square sections, starting in the corner farthest from the room's entrance. Load the roller with paint, and make a diagonal pass across the middle of the working area, then roll in parallel strokes through the diagonal line. This helps distribute the paint evenly for consistent coverage.

Move on to the next section as soon as the first is done, overlapping the wet edges of the first section before it dries. To help hide roller marks, work from the far corner to the room entry, and finish each section by rolling with strokes directed toward the entry wall. With a thorough, even coat on the ceiling, you can usually get by with one coat.

Roll the ceiling after cutting-in with a brush along the entire perimeter. A long extension pole for your roller makes ceiling work go much faster.

Latex or Oil Paint?

For standard wall and ceiling paint jobs, avoid using oil-base (alkyd) paint. Some pros still prefer alkyd paints for trim work and cabinets, but for interior surfaces, latex (water-base) paints are the way to go. Latex paints wash up with water, and their fumes are much less noxious during the drying process. Always use a nylon-bristle brush with latex paint; natural-bristle brushes are made for oil paints, which don't have water that can be sucked up by the bristles.

Sealing Stains

Common surface stains, including mildew, grease, wax, smoke, crayon, residue of oil-based adhesives, and discoloration from water damage, will show through ordinary primer and paint, no matter how many coats you put on. The best way to hide these stains is with a thorough coat of oil- or shellac-base primer/sealer. These run about $20 per gallon, usually around $7 more than a gallon of standard water-based primer. However, for the protection against stain bleed-through in messy rooms such as kid's rooms and kitchens, the extra expense is money well spent. The newest versions of these are made with odorless formulations and dry quickly.

Oil-base or shellac-base primers are messier to work with and require more clean up than latex-base, but they create a superior bonding surface for paint—not to mention blocking unsightly bleed-through. Interior-rated primer (left) should be used indoors. Use an exterior primer (right) for outdoor surfaces. Don't use them interchangeably.

Painting Trim

Window and door trim, baseboard, ceiling molding, and all other interior millwork looks best when painted with semi-gloss or gloss paint (also called enamel). These surfaces need the added durability and washability that comes with a glossy finish.

Paint color is an important consideration when it comes to trim. If you want the trim to pop out, choose a color that contrasts with the walls. For a more subtle, blended look, use the same or similar colors for the trim and walls.

To paint window and door trim, start at the top, then do the sides, and finish with the sill (on windows). If you over-brush onto the walls a little, you can cover up the marks when you paint the walls (paint trim first when possible). For most trim work, a 2½-inch angled sash brush works best, but for small trim pieces and window grilles, you might prefer using a 1½-inch sash brush.

When painting a window, never paint the tracks or any parts involved in the window operation.

Always paint trim with the grain of the wood (parallel to the length of the piece) to minimize brush marks. Be aware of joints where trim pieces meet and avoid leaving brush marks that cross against wood grain.

Extending Brush and Roller Life

If you're careless, the costs of rollers and brushes can add up on even a medium-sized paint job. When using latex paint, clean rollers and brushes thoroughly after painting, dry with a paper towel, and let them air dry completely before the next use. If you're using oil-based primers or paints, you can store paints and brushes, wrapped tightly in plastic wrap, in your freezer (they can stay there for months if need be). If you stop in the middle of project using latex paint, you can wrap paints and brushes in plastic and store them in the freezer for the next day—which will save you the hassle of cleaning them.

Painting Walls

If you're fixing up your house to live in, the walls can be your blank canvas for any color or treatment you desire. But if you're fixing up to sell, stick with the age-old real estate rule of neutrals—white (or any of the hundreds of variations on white), beige, or another soft, neutral tone. It may be boring, but neutral colors are safe, and that's the point. Many real estate pros also recommend using the same color throughout the living spaces, and why not? It makes it easier for you, and the buyers can (and likely will) repaint with their own colors.

Once you choose a color for your walls, decide on a sheen. Although flat is probably the most common choice, eggshell is generally considered the best all-around sheen for living spaces. It makes colors look good and is durable and reasonably washable without being too shiny. Flat paint is usually cheaper and has the benefit of hiding imperfections. If you choose flat, consider one of the newer "cleanable" types.

Before painting the walls, remove all switch plates, outlet covers, heat register covers, and anything else that shouldn't be painted. Tape over switches, outlets, and thermostats.

Make an N with a freshly loaded roller to begin each 3- to 4-ft. section, lifting the roller between each stroke. The first few passes unload the bulk of the paint onto the wall for even distribution.

Start by cutting in along the ceiling, wall corners, and next to all trim work. Roll the walls using a ¼- to ½-inch nap synthetic roller cover, depending on how much stippling you prefer; the deeper the nap, the more stippling you will get, resulting in a slight orange peel texture. Work in three-foot to four-foot-square sections, starting at the top of the wall. Then do the section just below before moving up and over to the next section, at the top again.

Proper wall-rolling technique saves time and paint. It starts with loading the roller fully in the paint tray, then going back and forth a few times along the tray's ridged ramp to distribute the paint. Make a diagonal pass from bottom to top of your square section. Lift the roller and make a vertical pass down from the top corner of the diagonal line. Lift again, then roll up from the bottom of the diagonal line with another vertical sweep to create an N. Fill in with horizontal sweeps, then make final, vertical sweeps to smooth out the roller marks.

Mind if I Cut In?

Cutting in is the trade term for freehand painting along an edge. Pros know that cutting in without the crutch of using masking tape gives you greater control of where the paint goes and is ultimately faster and easier. The trick is to fan out the brush close to the edge and essentially push the paint where you want it to go. It takes a little practice, but once you get the hang of it, you'll swear off tape forever.

Be sure to use a quality, nylon-bristle brush with a flagged edge, which means the bristle ends are split and cut to slightly different lengths to hold paint better. A 2½" angled sash brush is considered the best brush for most cutting-in.

Press the brush into the surface as you move it slowly, parallel to the edge. The bristles should bend in the middle and fan out at the ends so they nearly touch the cut-in edge. But because they don't actually touch, you'll see a fine line of paint getting pushed toward the edge as you move the brush. Follow that line with your eye, and adjust the brush accordingly to create the desired final line. Once the fine edge is established, you can brush less precisely to the side to create the 3-inch band that you'll overlap with the paint roller. Make sure the cut-in band completely hides the old paint, so you don't have to cut in again.

Don't overload the brush for cut-in work. Dipping into a small pail with 1" or less of paint will give you the right amount on the brush. Tap the brush against the sides of the pail before each stroke.

Fanning out the edge of the brush and moving with a slow, steady stroke are the keys to a clean cut-in line. Done correctly, the technique will produce a thin ridge of paint that flows from the brush and into the crevice at the point of intersection.

Floors

Flooring for living spaces runs the gamut from ceramic tile to lush carpeting. Cleaning, repairs, and replacement of vinyl and tile flooring are discussed in beginning of this book, so here we'll focus on the two materials you're most likely to have in your living spaces—carpet and wood. Plus, we'll discuss laminate plank flooring, which is arguably the best option for replacement flooring when a quick and easy upgrade is called for.

If you can't identify disgusting old carpeting with your eyes, you can usually spot it with your nose. Replace it before moving in whenever possible, and don't put your house on the market if your carpet looks like this.

How to Eliminate Floor Squeaks

If you can access floor joists from underneath, drive wood screws up through the subfloor to draw hardwood flooring and the subfloor together. Drill pilot holes and make certain the screws aren't long enough to break through the top of the floorboards. Determine the combined thickness of the floor and subfloor by measuring at cutouts for pipes.

When you can't reach the floor from underneath, surface-nail the floor boards to the subfloor with ring-shank flooring nails. Drill pilot holes close to the tongue-side edge of the board and drive the nails at a slight angle to increase their holding power. Whenever possible, nail into studs. Countersink the nails with a nail set and fill the holes with tinted wood putty.

Carpeting

Real estate agents frequently recommend replacing old carpets as part of prepping a home for sale. Carpeting looks most appealing to potential buyers (as well as guests) when the same material is used throughout the house, or throughout each floor in multistory homes. This often saves you money, too, because the cutoffs from large spaces may be used in smaller rooms, hallways, and entries.

If you've decided to replace your wall-to-wall carpeting, a midgrade carpet and pad are a safe choice for fixer-uppers in good condition.

Installing wall-to-wall carpeting properly is a considerable undertaking and one that most homeowners are better off hiring out to a qualified professional. If an installer is amenable to the idea, you can probably save a few bucks by tearing out the old carpet and pad yourself and vacuuming the subfloor so it's ready for the installation. This also gives you a chance to take care of squeaks by screwing loose areas of the subflooring to the floor joists below.

Removing conventional carpet is easy: With all of the furniture out of the way, grab a corner of the carpet with pliers and pull it away from the tackless strips along the wall. Roll the carpet back about four feet all the way down the room's longest wall, and cut through the backing (from the backside) with a sharp utility knife to remove a two- to three-foot-wide strip.

With the carpet removed, cut through the pad from the top and roll it up as well. Remove the pad's staples (there will be hundreds of them) from the subfloor with a scraper and pliers. Disposing of the old carpet and pad might take some finagling. Your trash service might take it, since it's in manageable rolls, or you can haul it to a dump yourself or try to work a deal with your carpet installer. Ask your installer about places where you can recycle the pad, which can save you some money and is a good thing to do for the environment.

● How to Remove Old Carpeting

Tacked carpet: Cut wall-to-wall carpeting into strips as you work to make removal and disposal easier.

Bonded carpet: Carpet that has been bonded to the floor or floor underlayment is a pain to remove. You may be better off removing and replacing underlayment rather than trying to salvage it.

Renewing Carpet

If carpet replacement isn't warranted or just doesn't fit into your budget, you should probably opt to have it professionally cleaned, or at the very least do it yourself with a rented machine.

If your carpet is largely fine, you may be able to get away with addressing just the problem areas. Localized spot damage, such as burn marks, marring an otherwise presentable carpet can often be repaired by cutting out the damaged area and filling in with a patch cut from a remnant of the same carpet.

But check with an expert at a carpet store first, because some carpets such as Berbers, are woven with long threads that extend well beyond the damaged area. Cutting any threads in these carpets can lead to serious unraveling.

To make a spot repair, you'll cut out the damaged area using a round cookie-cutter tool available at carpet stores. For larger areas, you'll need to cut a square-edged patch with a utility knife and glue it in place with carpet tape and seam adhesive.

If you simply want to renew the look of the entire carpet, steam cleaning machines are widely available for rent at supermarkets, home centers, and other retail stores. Using them is pretty straightforward: First, vacuum the carpet with your regular vacuum. Apply pretreatment solutions as needed to help eliminate tough stains. Steam machine companies offer their own cleaning products and can advise you on how to treat various common stains. Next, mix the general carpet-cleaning solution with tap water and pour it into the steam machine. Turn on the machine and pull it backward at an even, steady rate to steam clean the carpet. Steam cleaning tends to work best with one pass, but check with the store if you think really dirty areas could use a second pass (this isn't recommended with Berber and other loop-weave carpets).

Refreshing Carpet Inexpensively

If you prefer not to spend the money on renting a steam cleaner or hiring a professional to clean your carpets, you can still revive them with spot cleaning and an odor eliminating treatment. Start by treating spots with a general-purpose carpet spot remover (always blot, don't scrub because that can make the stain worse). Test any cleaner you use in an inconspicuous spot first to ensure it won't damage the carpet. After treating all the spots on the carpet, crush a handful of lavender—or other dried flower or herb with a mild scent that appeals to you—and mix with a cup of baking soda. Sprinkle the mixture across the carpet and then thoroughly vacuum.

How to Patch Damaged Carpeting

1 **Cut the damaged patch of carpet** out with a cookie-cutter tool and cut an identical patch from a scrap piece of carpet from an innocuous area such as the floor of a closet. Insert double-face carpet tape under the cutout, so it overlaps the patch borders.

2 **Press the patch into place.** Make sure the direction of the nap or pattern matches the existing carpet. To seal the seam and prevent unraveling, apply seam adhesive to the edges of the patch.

Variation: Before cutting out larger areas for patching, relieve the tension of the carpet you're repairing by nudging in toward the damage with a carpet knee-kicker, then tacking the carpet in place with a nail every 2 to 4". Nail through scrap strips of carpet laid face down to help protect and hold the surrounding carpet while you patch it.

How to Steam-Clean Carpet

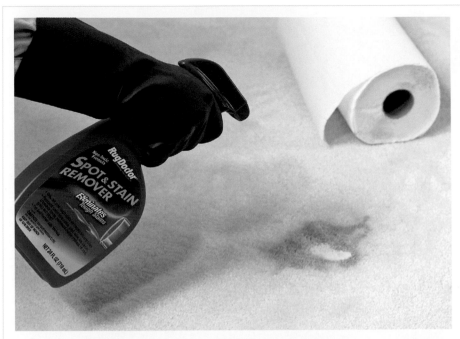

1 **Pre-treat any stains** with the manufacturer's recommended treatment, or another compatible cleaning solution, to get the best results with a rented steam cleaner.

2 **Move the cleaning machine** over the carpet as directed. It's best to complete the job with one pass, because multiple passes can overwet the carpet and pad.

Professional Carpet Cleaners

If you'd rather have your carpets cleaned by a pro, the best way to find a good cleaning service is to ask people you know for referrals. The carpet-cleaning business has more than its fair share of questionable practitioners, so it's important to find a company with a reputation for honest pricing and quality work. Most reputable businesses offer a solid, upfront quote based on measurements of your rooms and an initial consultation with you to discuss the services you want or need. Furniture moving, pre-cleaning treatments, and removal of ordinary stains typically are standard features. Be wary of low-ball, by-the-room rates, as well as extra charges for services that seem to be standard with other companies.

Wood Flooring

Real wood floors are coveted features in the home marketplace, and are almost always worth the expense of refinishing for a sale or for enjoying the floors for years to come. Aside from its undeniable beauty, perhaps the best feature of solid-wood flooring is how renewable it is. Even serious neglect and years of everyday wear and tear can be nearly or totally erased with a good sanding and careful refinishing. Boards with extensive damage can be replaced prior to refinishing. Minor repairs to scratches and isolated damage can improve the look of the floor and prevent further damage, but blending them in can be a challenge.

However, there is a limit to how many times a wood floor can be refinished. The sanding process removes anywhere from $\frac{1}{32}$ to $\frac{1}{8}$ inch of the wood. Solid hardwood flooring found in most homes can be sanded several times, while engineered wood flooring (a laminated material with a thin solid-wood top layer) can be sanded only one or two times in most cases.

Skilled do-it-yourselfers will find floor-sanding machines and sanding belts or pads at rental centers. The job needs to be done carefully, because in addition to being hard labor, it can be a bit tricky. For everyone else, professional floor refinishers are a good option. For around $2 to $3 per square foot, you'll usually get better results in much less time. Although several traditional and specialty finishes are available, most homeowners end up choosing clear polyurethane for its economy, durability, and ease of maintenance.

Refinishing hardwood floors is a labor-intensive and dirty DIY project that requires careful use of rental equipment for high-quality results. But even hiring a pro is an affordable solution.

Protecting Hardwood Floor Finishes

One of the best ways to prolong the life of your hardwood floor's finish is also the easiest: make the home a no-shoe area. Not only do shoes track in dirt and grime that can scratch and mar a finish, hard shoe soles are more likely than socks or bare feet to grind in scratches and degrade the finish. Professional floor refinishers estimate that this simple practice can add years to the life of your finish.

How to Clean a Hardwood Floor

1 Vacuum the entire floor. Mix hot water and dishwashing detergent that doesn't contain lye, trisodium phosphate, or ammonia. Working on 3-ft.-square sections, scrub the floor with a brush or nylon scrubbing pad. Wipe up the water and wax with a towel before moving to the next section.

2 If the water and detergent don't remove the old wax, use a hardwood floor cleaning kit. Use only solvent-type cleaners, as some water-based products can blacken wood. Apply the cleaner following the manufacturer's instructions.

3 When the floor is clean and dry, apply a high-quality floor wax. Paste wax is more difficult to apply than liquid floor wax, but it lasts much longer. Apply the wax by hand, then polish the floor with a rented buffing machine fitted with synthetic buffing pads.

Replacing a Floorboard

A single damaged floorboard can be replaced on your hardwood floors, but it isn't as simple a job as you might think. It involves removing the damaged board, finding a replacement that matches, and installing the new board. The trick lies in finding a good match and in altering the new board so it can fit into the tongue-and-groove installation system.

1 **Cut out the damaged portion** of the board using a combination of saws and chisels. Remove boards in full-width (tongue to groove) pieces.

2 **The replacement board** must be altered by cutting off the lower lip of the grooved edge so it can be fitted over the tongue at the edge of the repair area. Patches are fastened by face–nailing, and then covering the nail heads with tinted wood putty.

Lower lip has been removed

3 **Remove the lower lip** from the grooved edge of the replacement board by rapping the end of the lip with a sharp chisel and mallet.

4 **Install the patch board** or boards in the damaged area that has been cleared. Setting the patch with a light blow from a wood mallet is fine, but do not force the patch into the opening. If it doesn't fit, remove it and trim the edge slightly.

5 **Drive 4d finish nails** through the edges of the replacement board and into the subfloor. Drill pilot holes first. Cover the nail heads with wood putty and finish the patch to match the surrounding wood.

Laminate Flooring

When a room is crying out for new flooring, you really can't beat a laminate plank floor. Starting at $2 to $3 per square foot, laminate is one of the cheapest floor coverings you can buy, and it's very easy to install. It's also a great performer, thanks to its durable wear layer that resists scratches, dents, and stains and cleans up with a cloth or a damp mop.

Laminates are made with high-density fiberboard covered with a photo layer that can mimic everything from distressed, old-growth hardwood to marble tile. Cheaper versions are predominantly available in standard wood finishes, such as oak, maple, and cherry. The photo layer is protected by a clear wear layer on top, while another protective layer usually covers the bottom for added moisture protection. Overall thickness ranges from 6 mm to 12 mm, and 8 mm laminate is a good standard to shop for. Combined with the foam pad that cushions the flooring and allows it to "float" over the subfloor, the total installed thickness is about ⅜ inch.

You can lay laminate flooring directly over any standard subflooring, or over existing flooring, including solid or engineered wood, vinyl, tile, and concrete. However, the floor must be relatively level, smooth, and firmly affixed to the surface below it. For concrete floors, particularly those in basements and other below-grade locations, follow the laminate manufacturer's recommendations for installing a plastic moisture barrier below the new pad and flooring. Older versions of laminate (and a few current versions) were glued along the joints, but most types today simply snap together with special interlocking edges. This allows the flooring to be disassembled for moves, or for replacing damaged planks.

The installation process itself is remarkably easy and the flooring can be installed by the average do-it-yourselfer in less than a day, in the average room.

Here's an overview of the standard installation process: Unroll the manufacturer's recommended underlayment to cover the entire subfloor (some laminate planks come with underlayment attached). Tape the underlayment strips together, as directed. Starting at one long wall of the room, lay out the first row of planks, maintaining the specified expansion gap from the wall. Lay out the first pieces of the next row, beginning with a half-length plank, to create an offset for the end-joints between rows, and so on. As soon as you finish laying the floor, it's ready to walk on.

Laminate Floor Life

The key to getting the best value out of laminate flooring is avoiding damage that might cut its life short. The number one culprit of avoidable laminate floor damage is careless cleaning. Always sweep up loose dirt before cleaning and avoid general cleaners—they're usually too harsh and can quickly discolor the floor. Use cleaners specifically formulated for laminate flooring and apply the cleaner to a clean cloth rather than directly to the floor. However, the best cleaner for day-to-day spills and grime is a cloth moistened just with warm water.

Final uncut plank ends here

Strip laminate flooring is a thin, durable flooring that easily snaps together with interlocking joints at the edges and ends of the strips.

How to Install a Laminate Floor

1 **Lay out the first row of planks** along the starting wall. Use spacers to maintain expansion gaps (typically ⅜") along all walls. Lock the planks together at the ends.

2 **Use a drawbar,** available at home centers and flooring stores, to lock in the end joint for the final plank in each row.

3 **Continue to lay rows of planks,** locking all the edges together in a row, then locking the entire new row into the previous one. Make sure the joints are staggered by starting each row with a plank one-third the length of the previous row's starting plank.

4 **Fill in the last row.** Rip-cut planks as necessary to fit. Mark for cutting by placing the board backwards over the gap and marking where the edge should be. Rip-cut to width using a circular saw and straightedge guide, and cutting on the backside of the plank.

Electrical Upgrades

Whether you're a new buyer or a seller, a few simple upgrades can have a big impact on home design and performance. For example, replace the cover plates on all switches and electrical receptacles to add a nice fresh touch.

Swap out an old thermostat with a modern digital model to send a subtle message that your heating and cooling system is up to date. Add brand-new smoke alarms, even if the older ones still appear to be in working order.

Replacing a Thermostat

Replacing an old thermostat with a more efficient unit (especially if it is a programmable model) adds an updated look and energy efficiency that house hunters are likely to notice—as will you when you receive your lower utility bill. Be sure the new thermostat is compatible with your heating and cooling system. Basic programmable electronic thermostats start about $40.

To replace an old thermostat, turn off the power to the heating/cooling system at your home's main electrical service panel. Remove the thermostat's cover to expose the wiring and the mounting screws securing the thermostat body to the wall plate. Remove these screws and carefully pull off the thermostat body.

Thermostats are wired with color-coded, low-voltage wires (typically four) connected to screw terminals on the wall plate. Label each of these wires according to the letter next to its respective screw terminal. Loosen the screw terminals to free the wires. Tape the wire cable to the wall to keep them from slipping into the wall cavity, then unscrew the wall plate and set it aside.

Feed the cable through the wall plate of the new thermostat, and mount the plate to the wall. Connect each of the low-voltage wires to a screw terminal on the new unit, following the manufacturer's wiring diagram. Install the backup battery in the new thermostat body, and secure the body to the wall plate. Restore power to the system and test the thermostat.

Degrees of Expense

Lowering your thermostat by just two to three degrees can save you as much as $100 over a season's worth of cold weather (depending on the area you live in and the size of your home.)

How to Replace a Thermostat

1 **Examine the body of the thermostat** to see if it has a mercury switch, then remove the body to access the wiring.

2 **Connect the low-voltage wires** to the terminals on the new thermostat wall plate, then snap on the cover (inset) to complete the installation.

Decorative cover plates for switches and receptacles make a strong design statement for very little cost (ranging from $.50 for plain white plastic, to $5 to $8 for the fancy versions shown here). Plates for bathrooms and kitchens are often made with high-tech materials and a modern appearance. You'll find plenty of designer plates that fit better in formal living areas.

Installing Smoke Alarms

The local building code is the final authority on where you need smoke alarms in your house, but here are the most commonly required locations:

- Each story, including the basement (at least one alarm)
- Bedrooms
- Hallways adjoining bedrooms

If you're missing a working alarm in any of these areas, it's time to get one. In new home construction, smoke alarms typically must be wired together on a household circuit, so they're always armed (unless the power goes out, in which case a backup battery takes over), and they all go off simultaneously if one alarm is tripped. In existing homes, battery-powered alarms are generally acceptable.

Installing a battery-powered smoke alarm takes just a few minutes. Consult the manufacturer's instructions for proper placement (this is no time to ignore the fine print and wing it). Alarms aren't as effective when installed too close to ceiling fans, air registers, or wall-ceiling junctures, for example. Once you've marked the location, screw the mounting plate to the ceiling (or wall, as appropriate), load the battery into the body, then twist the body onto the mounting plate. Test the alarm, and you're done. Don't worry, your hearing will return to normal in a moment.

Smoke alarms are essential safety devices and are always included in home inspections. Most building codes allow battery-powered alarms in existing homes. Replacing all your alarms, even if they're working, is advisable. You must leave at least 4" of clearance between the alarm and any adjoining walls or the ceiling.

Warning

Many older thermostats have a small glass vial containing highly poisonous mercury liquid, which serves as its temperature-sensitive switch. Be very careful when handling a thermostat body with a mercury vial. Once removed, seal the body in a plastic bag and take it to a hazardous waste recycling facility (contact your city or county waste authority for facility locations). Do not discard the thermostat in your household trash.

Bettering Bedrooms

Bedrooms are typically among the simplest items on a fix-up checklist, usually calling for no more than a general freshening of paint, flooring, and possibly window treatments. But if you're showing your house for sale, it's important that the bedrooms look as spacious and inviting as possible.

Size and comfort notwithstanding, perhaps the most important aspect of a bedroom for both buyers and sellers may just turn out to be the closet. Years ago, house hunters paid little attention to closets, and home designers and builders considered storage spaces to be more perfunctory than primary considerations. But that's changed. Today's house hunters always check the closets, secretly hoping that the door will open onto a cavernous, uncluttered space that promises to hold every wearable

item they own. Your closets probably can't promise all that, but you can easily make a small closet more promising by installing an inexpensive closet organizer.

Economical vinyl-coated steel closet system parts are available piece-by-piece or in sets at any large home center. Ask a salesperson to help you choose the right pieces for your closet. Shelves, hanger bars, and prefabricated organizer units are made to hang on steel tracks that mount to the back wall of the closet. Whenever possible, designate some space for double-hanging clothes—with shirts and coats on top and pants below. Also include a full-length hanger section for dresses and long coats. Shoe organizers are great for clean and compact shoe storage, leaving the closet floor free and uncluttered.

With a little creative planning and a half-day's work, you can overhaul the storage space of a small closet for a very small investment.

Cleaning Living Areas

WALLS & CEILINGS

Painted surfaces: Remove ordinary stains by blotting with a cloth sprayed with all-purpose cleaner/disinfectant. Blot again with a sponge wetted with household cleaning powder mixed with hot water. Rinse with a damp cloth. Remove scuffs with a commercial sponge eraser (such as Mr. Clean Magic Eraser).

Wallpaper (vinyl): Remove dirt and ordinary stains by blotting with a cloth and solution of 1 teaspoon dish soap to 1 quart warm water. Remove scuffs and smudges with a commercial sponge eraser or a clean pencil eraser.

Wood paneling (painted): Remove dirt and ordinary stains by blotting with a cloth and solution of 1 teaspoon dish soap to 1 quart warm water. Blot again with an appropriate wood cleaner (such as for wood floors). Rinse with a damp cloth, then dry. Remove scuffs with a commercial sponge eraser.

WOOD TRIM

Paint or polyurethane finish: Remove beverage stains and cooking oil by blotting with a cloth and solution of 1 teaspoon dish soap to 1 quart warm water. Blot again with commercial wood cleaner, as directed. Wipe dry. Remove water stains by blotting with a cotton cloth and solution of 1 teaspoon dish soap to 1 quart warm water; buff with a dry cloth. Scrape up hardened wax with a plastic scraper or credit card, then wipe with a damp cloth, and buff with a dry cloth.

Oil finish: Remove beverage stains and cooking oil by blotting with a cloth and solution of 1 teaspoon dish soap to 1 quart warm water. Blot again with commercial wood cleaner, as directed. Wipe dry. Remove water stains by rubbing with mineral spirits and fine steel wool (rub with the grain). Buff with a dry cloth. Scrape up hardened wax with a credit card, then blot with a 1-to-1 paste of baking soda and water. Wipe with a damp cloth, and buff with a dry cloth.

Shellac (varnish) finish: Remove beverage and food stains with furniture polish, as directed. Remove water stains by blotting with solution of 1 part mineral spirits, 1 part raw linseed oil, and a small amount of white vinegar.

FLOORS

Carpet (synthetic fiber): *Note: Test all cleaning solutions on a carpet remnant to check for color-fastness and staining.* Remove common stains (including crayon, permanent marker, ink, chewing gum, wax, and butter) by applying a small amount of non-acetone nail polish remover (or another oil solvent) to a cloth and blot. Rinse with a spray of water, then blot dry. Remove beverage and pet stains by blotting with solution of 1 teaspoon dish soap to 1 quart warm water. After 15 minutes, blot with 1-to-1 solution of white vinegar and water. After 15 minutes, blot with damp cloth and let dry.

Wood (polyurethane finish): Remove cooking oil and crayon by blotting with hydrogen peroxide solution applied to a cloth. Blot again with commercial wood cleaner, as directed. Remove beverage stains, pet stains, chewing gum residue, and wax by blotting with commercial wood cleaner, as directed. Remove scuffs with a commercial sponge eraser. *Note: Oil soap, floor wax, and other products may preclude the option of recoating polyurethane finishes.*

Laminate: Remove beverage stains, grease, and chocolate with cloth and laminate floor cleaner, as directed. Remove tar, shoe polish, paint, ink, crayon, and nail polish with rubbing alcohol or nail polish remover applied to a cloth. Remove hardened wax and chewing gum by scraping gently with a plastic scraper. *Note: Consult the flooring's manufacturer for specific cleaning recommendations.*

Apply stain remover to a clean, dry cloth and rub lightly to remove the stain.

Seal all stain areas with white pigmented shellac. Pigmented shellac prevents stains from bleeding through the new paint.

Water or rust stains may indicate water damage. Check for leaking pipes and soft plaster, make needed repairs, then seal the area with stain-killing sealer.

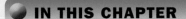
Doors and Windows

A house really has only two kinds of moving parts: doors and windows. And that's a good thing, because all moving parts sooner or later end up with problems. Chances are you know exactly which doors and windows are giving you trouble at the moment. What you may not care to recall is exactly how many dozens of times you've intended to fix each of those problem parts, and perhaps you don't know how. This chapter will help with the how-to information; you'll find it's more about motivation than about any significant expense.

If you're selling your home, you may have asked yourself, "Do I really need to fix something as insignificant as a sticking door or a torn screen?" The answer is yes, for the same reason that you patch a hole in the driveway or trim an overgrown shrub: You want the house to look like it has been well cared for over the years, and that you're not trying to pawn off minor problems onto the home's new owners. On the other hand, if you happen to be a new owner who has inherited some nagging door and window problems, now's the time to make a fresh start and show the world that you're not the type who leaves such nuisances to posterity.

Of course, there's more to fixing up doors and windows than basic repairs and maintenance. One of the primary house features house hunters notice is the main entry door. The presentation of the front door is an important sign of welcome, and an attractive entry is like a friendly greeting, while an unappealing one is a sure way to start off on the wrong foot. So we've included some simple projects and upgrades to give your home's facade a winning smile.

◯ Doors

The key to doctoring doors is an accurate diagnosis. You already know the symptoms—the door rubs against the jamb when it closes, or it won't latch, or you have to put your shoulder into it to get it to stay closed, or whatever—now you have to figure out what's causing the problem. The illustration on page 83 points to the most common door ailments and their usual causes. The following pages show you how to administer specific treatments.

Fixing Hinges

Most door problems start with the hinges. By far the most common door ailment is a loose top hinge, for which gravity is mostly to blame. Hinges are held in place by screws driven into the door jamb, which is typically made of ¾-inch softwood ill equipped to support the weight of a door over many years. When the top-hinge screws loosen, the door hangs askew in its opening, eventually rubbing against the latch-side jamb and/or the floor or threshold. To determine if this is your problem, open the door a few inches, and lift up on the knob to see whether the door moves toward the hinge jamb. If so, try tightening the screws on all of the hinges.

If the hinge screws don't hold any more, replace one or more of the old screws with a 2½- or 3-inch wood screw, to fasten the hinge not just to the jamb but also the stud behind the jamb. Replace the screws one at a time, and drill pilot holes so you don't split the jamb.

If a hinge leaf has come loose from the door, you can replace the original screws with longer ones if the door frame is solid wood. With hollow-core doors, longer screws won't help. Instead,

A door that is in poor repair, or even simply outdated, gives exactly the wrong first impression to visitors and potential buyers alike. Making simple repairs to the door and frame and upgrading the lockset and deadbolt are easy, inexpensive solutions.

apply a little epoxy filler into the screws holes, then re-install the screws. Support the weight of the door while the epoxy cures.

Another common problem is a bent top hinge that allows the door to lean toward the latch jamb. To correct this, remove the hinge pin from the offending hinge. Grab each knuckle of the bent hinge leaf with an adjustable wrench and bend it back into shape. Most hinges have a little bit of play in them, so you can bend a little extra in either direction to adjust the gap between the door and jambs. If you bend too much, the pin won't go back in. Replace the pin and test the door's fit and operation.

If a door binds against the hinge-side jamb, it's usually because the hinge leaf is set too deeply into its mortise, so that the door edge is compressed against the jamb when the door closes. Remove the hinge screws and place a thin cardboard shim between the hinge leaf and the jamb.

● How to Fix Door Hinge Problems

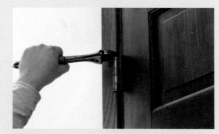

Long screws driven into the framing secure a loose hinge and pull the door toward the hinge-side jamb. Screws closer to the wall surface tend to hit the drywall instead of the wall studs.

Hinges or hinge pins that are bent have a negative impact on door operation. Remove the hinge pin with pliers or an adjustable wrench so you can inspect the parts. If either a leaf of the plate or the pin itself is bent, straighten it in a vise.

Adjust the door if it is binding on the hinge side by bending the hinge slightly. One quick way to do this is to insert the butt of a nailset between the leaves and then draw the door shut, causing the tops of the leaves to bend slightly. Take care not to do this too fast or too long.

Door Trouble Spots

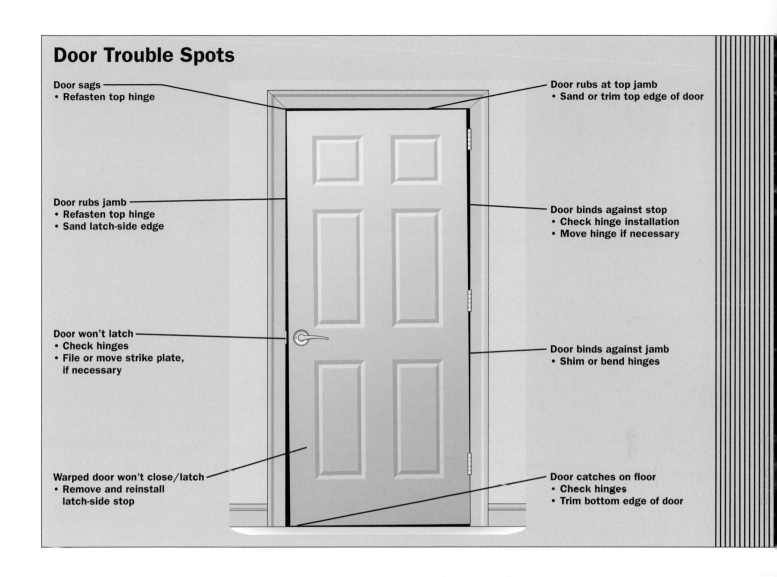

Door sags
- Refasten top hinge

Door rubs jamb
- Refasten top hinge
- Sand latch-side edge

Door won't latch
- Check hinges
- File or move strike plate, if necessary

Warped door won't close/latch
- Remove and reinstall latch-side stop

Door rubs at top jamb
- Sand or trim top edge of door

Door binds against stop
- Check hinge installation
- Move hinge if necessary

Door binds against jamb
- Shim or bend hinges

Door catches on floor
- Check hinges
- Trim bottom edge of door

The Door to Energy Savings

Drafty exterior doors can cost you hundreds of dollars a year in unnecessary heating and cooling costs. Fortunately, weatherizing your doors to make the home more energy efficient is a cheap and easy upgrade. Add felt strips to the edge of the jamb doorstop on the exterior side (about $3 a roll), and attach new door sweeps (at right, about $10) to the bottom of doors on the interior side (use felt or bristle sweeps over uneven floors).

Freeing Sticking Doors

This common household malady is often caused by humidity, as wood doors swell with moisture until they rub against their jambs. In other sticky cases, the door frames get out of whack due to settling of the surrounding structural elements.

If the door sticks at the top or bottom, sand the appropriate edge of the door with coarse sandpaper. This may be all you need for a minor problem. But if you have to remove more than ⅟₃₂ inch or so, it will be faster cut the door with a circular saw.

When cutting a door with a saw, place a piece of hardboard or cardboard over the door to prevent the saw foot from marking or scratching the door. Round over the cut edges with a file or sandpaper, then paint or finish the bare edge to match the existing finish (this is important to prevent future swelling from moisture).

Solving Latch Problems

Doors don't properly close and latch when the bolt isn't lined up with the strike plate hole (the strike plate is the flat, metal plate mortised into the door jamb). To diagnose the problem, mark the location of the bolt onto the door jamb or edge of the strike plate, then compare the marks to the hole in the strike plate to see whether the bolt is too high or too low. If it's too low, check the top door hinge to see if it can be drawn more tightly against the jamb by driving in long screws (page 82). If it's too high, make sure the bottom hinge was installed properly, and make any necessary adjustments.

If the hinges are flush and securely fastened, turn your attention to the strike plate trying the solutions shown on this page. If the bolt seems to be aligned with the strike plate's hole, it could be that the door isn't closing far enough for the bolt to reach the hole. Check this by closing the door and watching what the bolt does. Will it engage the hole if you push the door hard? If so, remove the strike plate and bend the little tab on the inside of the hole. If that doesn't do the trick, you can move the strike plate away from the stop. It's best to move it at least ¼ inch, so the strike plate screws won't slip back into the old holes. Another common cause of this problem is a warped door. The easiest fix for that is to move the stop (see page 85).

● How to Fix Latch Misalignment

Correct minor strike bolt alignment problems by filing the top or bottom edge of the strike-plate opening.

Fix severely misaligned latches by moving the strike plate so it aligns with the bolt. You may have to drill into the jamb to enlarge the counterbore for the bolt, and you will have to expand the mortise with a chisel so the strike plate sits flush. You can fill in the exposed area of the original mortise with wood filler.

Tip: Quick Fix for Squeaky Doors

Stopping a squeak is the easiest repair in the book: Spray the knuckles of the offending hinge (or better yet, spray all of them) with a penetrating lubricant such as WD-40. Wipe up any drips or overspray with a rag. Open and close the door a few times to distribute the lubricant.

Trim doors to length with a circular saw and straightedge guide. To prevent splintering, score the cutting line with a utility knife. Clamp a straightedge to the door to keep the saw from drifting during the cut.

If your door is binding in the door frame, one solution is to plane or trim it to fit into an opening that has fallen out of square. Use a compass to scribe the edge of the opening onto the door in the area where it is binding. Then, remove the door and trim it with a plane or by cutting with a saw.

● How to Adjust for a Warped Door

Stop

1 **Warped doors are hard to correct.** It's easier to move the stop, and no one will ever notice the difference.

2 **Push the stop up against the closed door,** then back it off slightly before nailing it with finish nails.

Tuning Up Sliding Doors

While you may be accustomed to your pesky sliding glass door, prospective buyers won't be impressed if they throw their backs out trying to wrench it open. Here's how you can give a sliding door a 10-minute tune-up. First, clean the tracks with a screwdriver and then use a vacuum cleaner to remove accumulated dirt and grime. Wipe down the metal with a rag and all-purpose cleaner (such as Formula 409) or degreaser. Clean both the top and bottom tracks on both sides of the door.

Next, spray the tracks with a light coat of penetrating lubricant such as WD-40. Use the sprayer tube to inject lube onto the wheels inside the door. Open and close the door several times to see if it operates smoothly. If not, check to see if the wheel adjustment is causing rubbing or binding along the top and/or bottom track. Experiment with the wheel adjustment until the door runs smoothly. Wipe up excess lubricant so it won't attract dirt. Finally, spray inside the keyhole or lock mechanism and operate the lock several times to distribute the lube.

Most sliding doors have screws on the side or back edges that raise or lower the wheels. Turn the screws to level the door and keep it from rubbing along the tracks.

Doorknobs, Locksets & Deadbolts

There isn't much that goes wrong with doorknobs that a little spray lubricant can't fix. If a handle is sticking or a deadbolt is stiff, spray penetrating lubricant (don't use graphite) into the keyholes and around the bolt. Run the key in and out a few times and turn the lock and handle repeatedly to loosen everything up. Wipe up any overspray runoff immediately, to prevent staining.

If a doorknob or lock still won't turn, try slightly loosening the mounting bolts. The bolts pull the halves of the lockset together, and they can cause the handle to bind if they're too tight.

If a lockset is acting up so much that you're considering taking it apart, it's probably time to replace it. A new lockset can dress up an ordinary door surprisingly well. That said, if you're upgrading one doorknob on an interior door, it will look funny if the new one doesn't match the knobs on all the other interior doors.

Replacing a lockset takes only a few minutes. Use a small, flathead screwdriver to pop off any decorative covers or escutcheons, exposing the two mounting bolts. Remove the bolts and slide out the two halves of the set. Take out the screws securing the latch bolt's mounting plate to the edge of the door and pull out the bolt assembly. Insert the new latch bolt into the door edge to check the fit. If necessary, reshape the bolt mortise to accommodate the new mounting plate, using a sharp wood chisel.

With the outside face of the bolt plate flush with the door edge, screw it down with the provided screws. Insert the knob with the mounting-bolt sleeves through the holes in the latch bolt assembly, then position the other knob so the mounting bolt holes line up with the sleeves. Connect the two sides with the mounting bolts, tightening carefully and evenly. If the handles don't turn easily, loosen the tension on the mounting bolts. On some locksets, you have to install the covers and knobs before you can test the action.

Deadbolt Value

A bargain deadbolt is often more of an invitation to a burglar than any kind of real bargain. To ensure you're getting the safety you pay for with your deadbolt, look for an American National Standards Institute (ANSI) rating of grade 1. Other particulars to look for when considering potential deadlock purchases are: a "throw" (lock bolt penetration into the jamb) of 1" or longer; a saw-resistant bolt; hardened case steel housing and construction; and anti-drill features inside the lock housing. You'll recoup the modest additional cost for these features in added peace of mind.

How to Install a Deadbolt

1 **Position the supplied template** for the deadbolt and mark the hole locations. Use the size holesaw indicated in the deadbolt instructions, boring through the door until you break through the other side. Drill the other side to remove the remaining waste material.

2 **Drill the bolt hole** through the door edge with a spade bit. Keep the bit level. Push the bolt assembly into the hole so that the plate is flat against the door edge. Trace around the plate with a utility knife, remove mechanism, and cut a ⅛"-deep mortise into the door edge with a sharp chisel. Screw the bolt mechanism into place on the door edge, and screw both halves of the lock into place.

Jamb

Bolt hole

Stop

3 **Extend the lock bolt** and color the end with a grease pencil. Retract the bolt, close the door and extend the bolt so that it's end hits the jamb. Drill a bolt hole at that mark, 1½" deep, using a spade bit.

4 **Close the door and test the deadbolt.** If it doesn't fit into the hole, enlarge the hole slightly. Center the strike plate over the bolt hole and trace around it with a utility knife. Cut a mortise for the strike plate and screw the plate in place.

How to Install a Prehung Interior Door

1 **Set the door in the framed opening** with the door closed. Shift it so it is centered side to side and the jambs are flush with the wall surface. Check for plumb by placing a level on the hinge side jamb. Shim as necessary and then open the door—the pressure from the shims should hold the door in place.

2 **Anchor the hinge-side jamb** with 8d casing nails driven through the jamb and shims and into the rough frame. If the jambs are made of hardwood such as oak, drill pilot holes for the nails.

3 **Drive nails near the bottom hinge** and then the middle, if your door has three hinges. Make sure to drive through shims. If you drive nails away form the shims the jambs may bow outward.

4 **Double-check the jamb** on the strike plate side to make sure it is plumb and flush with the wall surface, and then nail it to the framing, nailing through the shims as you did on the hinge jamb.

5 **Drive a few nails** through pilot holes in the center of the door stop for reinforcement. Locate the nails so they go through shims.

6 **Attach the preattached case moldings** to the framing members with 4d finish nails. Set the nail heads. Fill all nail holes with wood putty and then paint or stain. Use a nail set to recess the nail heads. Install a latch set.

The All-important Entry Door

The main entry offers visitors a glimpse of the homeowner's taste and style and a hint at what awaits them inside. That's why any real estate agent will tell you that the front door is an important part of your home's curb appeal.

Replacing a front door is necessary only if the old one is severely warped, weather-beaten, damaged, or if it bears any telltale marks of a break-in. It's possible to replace just the door itself and not the jambs. But the easier approach is to replace the entire package with a new prehung door unit, which includes everything but the lockset. You may choose to do a simple one-for-one swap, or go ahead and install an impressive entry door system with sidelights and more (as in the photo on this page). Either way, the basic process involves tearing out the old door and its frame, enlarging the opening if need be, replacing the weatherproofing materials that protect the wall framing, and installing and finishing the new unit.

But you don't need to replace a door to make sure your entry sends a warm message of welcome. Take a step back and consider the whole package—the door, the light fixtures, the doorbell button, and the house numbers and mailbox (if they're part of the composition). Also look at the porch floor or stoop below the door. Is there a welcome mat? Is there room at either side of the door for a pot of flowers or other homey touches? By all means, the entry should be neat and orderly, with a full, unobstructed view of the door, but small chairs or modest decorations to the side help to soften and personalize the space.

If your door is in good condition and works well, it may need only some new paint to look great. When painting a door, choose exterior enamel paint, and be sure to also paint the doorframe and brick molding. Real estate folks commonly recommend using an accent color for a front door, especially for drab facades that could use some "character building."

Another trick is to add a brass kickplate to the bottom of the door. This can be an easy way to hide dings and pet scratches, but it's not the right look for every type of door. If necessary, replace the lockset and/or deadbolt. However, front door locksets can be pricey, so you might opt to buff up the old one if it still works well.

Before

After

The added curb appeal from an entry makeover can be one of the major elements that seals a home sale.

Installing a Storm Door

Storm doors protect an entry door from driving rain or snow, but they are also a quick and inexpensive solution if your front or back door doesn't look very appealing. Functionally, they create a dead air buffer between the two doors that acts like insulation. When the screen panels are in place, the door allows ventilation on a hot day. And they deliver a small measure of added security, especially when outfitted with a lockset and deadbolt lock.

Storm doors come in many different styles to suit just about anyone's design needs, ranging in price from basic (fairly flimsy) units for around $70 up to handsome models with every option imaginable for as much as $500. They come in many different types of materials, including aluminum, vinyl, wood and even fiberglass. You'll find that most units are fitted with full or nearly full glass exposure (half-panel storm doors are more efficient, but less popular). Higher end models include sliding panels that make switching from glass to screen a cinch.

Most units these days are prehung. Installation instructions vary, so be sure to check the manufacturer's directions. Regardless of the installation process, though, you should start by adding drip cap molding at the top of the door opening (unless otherwise indicated in the manufacturer's instructions).

Cold Comfort

Storm doors are intended as both protection against the elements and additional insulation against low temperatures. But when it comes to insulating values, not all storm doors are created equal. If you live in a colder part of the country and you're looking for a storm door that will help keep your energy bills as low as possible, look for an insulated unit. The best of these feature half panels of glass to decrease exposure and a thick bottom panel and rails crafted of insulating materials.

Getting extra insulating power from a storm door doesn't mean giving up design style, as this unit proves.

Door Closers

Storm doors are relatively lightweight, and because they open outward they are susceptible to catching the wind and becoming damaged. For this reason, a storm door should be equipped with a spring-protected safety chain at the top, and a pneumatic closer that can be located anywhere on the door (usually about handle level).

A quality storm door helps seal out cold drafts, keeps rain and snow off your entry door, and lets a bug-free breeze into your home when you want one.

How to Install a Storm Door

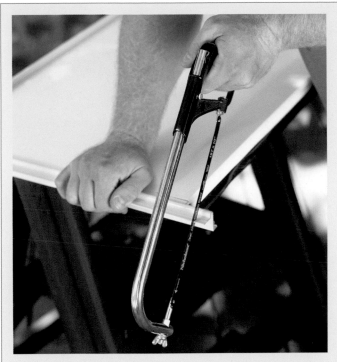

Test-fit the door in the opening. If it's loose, add a shim to the hinge side of the door, flush with the front of the casing. Measure the height of the door opening and cut hinge flanges to length with a hacksaw.

Set the door in place and partially drive mounting screws near bottom and top. Check for plumb and, when you're sure, screw the hinge-side flange to the casing.

Cut the latch-side flange with the hacksaw and attach it with two screws. Check for parallel to the hinge-side flange. Once you're satisfied with the fit, screw the latch-side flange to the casing. Install the door sweep on the bottom of the door.

Slide the outside of the lockset into the mounting holes and tape it into place. Screw the inside half of the lockset to the outside and tighten the screws securely. Install the deadbolt if the door has one and install the door closer and safety chain, and adjust to proper tension.

Fixing or Installing a Doorbell

A dead doorbell is a dead giveaway that your house needs some attention. It's worth spending a little time getting a failed chime up and running again, or simply replacing it with a new wireless unit.

Conventional wired doorbell systems have a few main parts: the switch (or button), the chime unit, and the transformer that steps down the 120-volt household electrical current to 24 volts or less. Thin, low-voltage wires connect the parts from the transformer.

To find out where a doorbell problem lies, start with the easy stuff first. Turn off the power at the main electrical service panel and check that the switch is still connected and not corroded or otherwise damaged by the elements. Next, inspect the chime unit. If the unit has real chimes that ring mechanically—that is, the tones aren't created electronically—clean the little pistons, or "plungers," that strike the chimes. These can get gummed-up so badly that they stick in one position. Clean the pistons and

springs with a cotton swab dipped in rubbing alcohol. Restore power to the system and test it.

At this point, if you still have a dead doorbell on your hands, you can either replace the wired switch and chime (try one first and then the other) or go the easier route and buy a new wireless unit that installs in about 10 minutes. You can find a quality wireless system for around $20, twice what the most basic wired system will run.

Ringing in Savings

When it comes to doorbells, the simpler the better. Very few prospective buyers—or just people in general—are impressed by a grand doorbell ring. And the mechanism itself is so basic, that this is definitely a case where shopping strictly by price is a good idea.

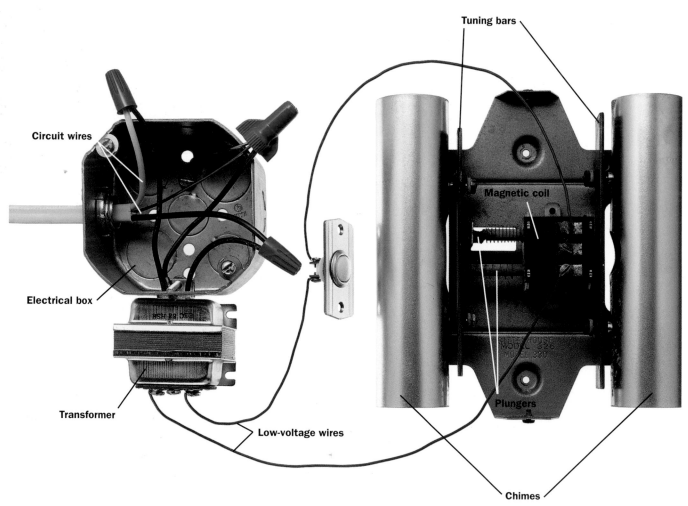

A home doorbell system is powered by a transformer that reduces 120-volt current to low-voltage current of 24 volts or less. Current flows from the transformer to one or more push-button switches. When pushed, the switch activates a magnet coil inside the chime unit, causing a plunger to strike a musical tuning bar.

How to Test a Doorbell

Start by testing all of the doorbell parts for loose wire connections. These parts include the switch (left photo), low-voltage transformer (middle photo), and the chime unit (right photo). The button and chime should be easy to access. The transformer is normally located in (or attached to) an electrical box in a wall or ceiling near the doorbell system.

Wireless Doorbells

Plug-in, wireless chime units can be plugged into any standard receptacle near the entry door, while battery-powered units offer more flexibility with placement. If you are replacing an old wired doorbell, be sure and disconnect the old transformer from the power source. When shopping for a new wireless doorbell, compare products for their transmission range, features, and sound quality. Basic systems come with one or two remote buttons and a plug-in or battery-powered unit. Mount the button to the wall next to the entry door (or doors), then plug in or mount the chime unit inside the house, making sure it's within the recommended transmission range.

A battery-powered wireless doorbell system includes a button with a transmitter, and a chime unit with a receiver.

How to Replace a Doorbell Switch

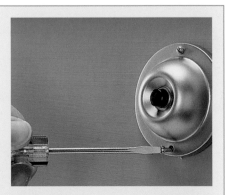

1 **Remove the doorbell switch** mounting screws, and carefully pull the switch away from the wall.

2 **Disconnect wires from the switch.** Tape wires to the wall to prevent them from slipping into the wall cavity.

3 **Purchase a new doorbell switch,** and connect wires to screw terminals on new switch. (Wires are interchangeable and can be connected to either terminal.) Anchor the switch to the wall.

Windows

Like doors, windows tend to get much less maintenance than they should. Nevertheless, most of them hold up pretty well over the years and can be tuned up nicely with a little attention and some inexpensive replacement parts. For a basic home fix-up, plan on cleaning all of your windows and freeing any stuck ones. Also replace any broken panes and torn screens, both of which are glaring symbols of neglect. All of these projects are covered here.

Freeing Stuck Windows

If you have a window that has been painted shut, begin to free it by cutting through the paint along the edges of the window sash using a utility knife, a putty knife, or a window zipper—a tool made specifically for this purpose. Tap around the sash frame with a hammer and a wood block, then cross your fingers and give the window a jerk. Repeat the tapping and jerking until the window gives. If all else fails, pry up the sash with a thin pry bar, but you may have to repair the wood later. Next, sand the paint inside the window tracks with fine sandpaper, and when you tire of that, wipe off the dust, then rub the tracks with a piece of wax candle to provide some lubrication.

To smooth the action on aluminum windows and storm units, clean the tracks with a toothbrush and a vacuum with a crevice attachment, and remove any stubborn gunk with a rag and all-purpose cleaner. Try the window to see if it moves satisfactorily. If not, spray the tracks with a little WD-40 or similar lubricant, and wipe up any excess. It's preferable to avoid using lubricant, since it attracts more dirt than bare metal, but sometimes lube is necessary.

A window that is in need of help usually is not shy about displaying warning signs. In some cases, a little weatherstripping or a new storm window is all that is needed.

A window zipper has only one job: to release windows that have been painted shut.

Stubborn windows may require a little persuasion to unstick. After cutting paint seals, tap (carefully) along the sash frame with a hammer and wood block.

A white candle or block of paraffin wax is an all-purpose lubricant for wood windows. Never use liquid or greasy lubricants on wood windows.

Improving Double-Hung Window Function

To determine the type of tension device in your double-hung window, inspect the sash tracks. Spring-loaded tensioners may have an adjustment screw. Some older spring types have a metal tube on the inside of each track. The tube contains a spring that is wound by twisting the tube itself. To adjust these, grip the tube tightly to prevent it from unwinding, then remove the screw near the top end of the tube. Turn the tube clockwise to increase the spring tension or counterclockwise to decrease tension. Replace the screw and test the window operation. Finally, newer windows with vinyl tracks may have spring-tensioned tracks that can be adjusted via screws hidden behind cap pieces somewhere along the track.

Older double-hung windows employ a pulley system that counterbalances the sash with weights hanging in cavities (called weight pockets) behind the window tracks. These are easily identifiable by the ropes running up from the sash and over a pulley at the top of each track. The pulley system is so simple it almost never wears out, but the ropes can break.

To repair an old pulley system, pry off the stops at the sides of the window sash, then remove the lower sash and set it aside. This gives you access to the cover that conceals the weight pocket. Pry off or unfasten the cover piece and pull out the weight from the pocket. Tie a small weight, such as a nail, to the end of a new sash cord and thread the cord over the pulley and down through the pocket opening. Re-tie the weight and set it back into the pocket. Reinstall the pocket cover.

Next, set the window sash onto the sill. Pull the cord until the weight nearly touches the pulley. Cut the cord to length, knot the end, and fit the knot into the edge of the sash frame. Install the sash and stops. To replace a cord for the upper sash, remove the parting stop between the two sashes, then remove the upper sash to access its weight pocket.

Replace or Repair?

Replacing all your single-pane double-hung windows with new insulated-pane models will cost you thousands of dollars. If you're updating for home sale, you should be aware that the National Association of Realtors estimates you recoup only half or less of that cost in resale value. Refurbishing the existing units may be the wiser course of action. If, however, the windows are timeworn and extremely drafty, and you plan on living in the house for a long time, new windows may eventually pay for themselves in savings on your energy bill.

● How to Service Double-Hung Windows

Look for adjustment screws inside the tracks (or sometimes behind the tracks) of single- and double-hung windows. Adjust both sides evenly to balance the sash movement.

Tube-type balancers have a spiraling spring inside a metal tube. The tube is secured with screws at the top and bottom ends and is always under tension.

Casement Windows

Casement widows have a metal crank mechanism that opens and closes the window. They do not have a good track record for durability. Eventually, the opening mechanism wears out and the window won't open or close without considerable assistance. You might be able to find a replacement handle at a local home center or hardware store. Beyond that, the only way to fix a bad crank is by replacing the whole mechanism. The window's manufacturer may offer replacement cranks for specific models, or check out online sources for hard-to-find window parts.

Lubricate the track and hinges on a casement window crank as part of your routine maintenance. Detach the extension arm from the bottom sash track so you can get access to the channel knob that fits into the track.

Channel knob

Casement window cranks are held in place with a few screws. Sometimes a crank is partially hidden under a trim piece screwed to the sill. The crank assembly can be removed and cleaned or replaced.

The Miniblind Solution

Completely bare windows can make a house look unfinished, even deserted. At the same time, it rarely makes sense to spend the money on fancy window treatments if you're selling your home, and elegant drapery isn't usually at the top of most new homeowners' fix-up lists.

So what's a fixer-upper to do with bare windows? Vinyl miniblinds. Depending on size and material, they run from $5 to about $30, so they're well within most any homeowner's budget. They're completely neutral from a decorating perspective, and easy to install. You can even shorten the length of a blind or trim a little off the ends if your window's too narrow. Miniblinds can be hung inside the window frame or on the trim or wall above the window. Install on the inside whenever possible, since trimwork is much more attractive than plastic blinds. Because the width is a more critical measurement when installing the blinds on the inside of the frame, you may have to order a custom size blind (cutting stock sizes to width yourself never works out well). If mounting on the frame or above the window, look for the narrowest available width that conceals the entire window pane.

Two brackets and four screws (included) are all it takes to add new miniblinds for a pleasingly neutral window treatment.

Replacing Window Glass

The proper technique for replacing a broken window pane depends on the type of window you have. Traditional divided-light windows have individual panes set into a framework of wood muntin bars and are secured with glazier's points and putty called glazing compound. Most older windows have a similar construction. Modern divided-light windows often have a single, large pane with a faux muntin frame that overlays the glass, or in some cases is installed between the glass panes. Replacing panes in sealed, insulated windows should be done by a professional to maintain the window's thermal performance.

To replace a glass pane on a traditional window, first remove any shards of broken glass, then follow the steps below, being careful not to break glass as you work.

Improving Older Windows

You don't have to replace your older windows to save hundreds on energy costs. Over time, glazing putty can crack, which allows for great thermal transfer between inside and out, bumping up your heating and cooling costs in the process. Simply re-glazing existing window panes (and re-caulking the window frames) in older homes can radically affect energy efficiency and save you a bundle of cash with very little effort.

● How to Replace a Glass Pane

1 **Soften old glazing putty** with a heat gun set on medium or low, being careful not to scorch the wood. If the heat doesn't work, coat the compound with linseed oil and let sit. The oil will eventually soften the putty.

2 **Remove softened putty** with a putty knife. Repeat in small sections until all the putty is removed, and remove any old glazier points still in the frame. Scrape the edges clean and coat the bare wood with primer.

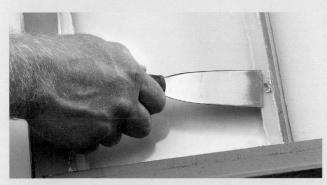

3 **Measure the inside dimensions** of the frame and order a replacement pane about ⅛" smaller in width and height than the opening. Make a bed for the pane with a thin bead of glazing putty inside the frame, and seat the glass securely in it to ensure a good seal. Drive glazier's points into each side of the frame with a putty knife blade to secure the new pane.

4 **Lay another, thicker bead of putty** along the pane's edges, then smooth it into a clean bevel with a putty knife. Clean off any excess and let dry as directed. Prime and then paint the putty and frame edges to match the rest of the window.

Window Screening

Installing new window screening can be a little frustrating until you get the hang of it, but the materials are inexpensive and the work is, ultimately, easy. Standard window screen (technically called insect mesh) is made of fiberglass or aluminum, both of which come in black, silver, and grayish tones. Black tends to offer the best visibility and least glare, but it makes sense to match whatever you have on the other screens in the house. Keep in mind that aluminum will oxidize in coastal climates. Rolls of screening, vinyl spline (the solid tubing that holds in the screen), and spline rollers (an essential efficiency tool) are available at any home center or hardware store. Better still, purchase a screen repair kit with all those materials in one handy bag, for between $10 and $15.

The majority of window screens today are aluminum or vinyl frames with the screen secured by rubber spline that runs in a channel around the edges of the frame. When replacing the screen, both the spline and old damaged screen are removed and discarded.

Some older homes have wood window screen frames. Changing screening in these frames involves removing an inner trim piece, and pulling out staples that hold the screen, then stapling in a new one.

Minor Screen Repairs

It's amazing how mosquitoes and flies can find the smallest of holes in a screen. But that doesn't mean you need to replace the whole screen. For minor tears or holes where the screen wires or fabric are still intact, you can do a spot repair. Simply lay the screen on a flat work surface and flatten out the wires around the damaged area to their original position. Then apply a thin bead of super glue or rubber cement (even clear nail polish will work) along the line of the tear or the hole. The result will be an inexpensive and invisible repair that keeps the insects on the outside, where they belong.

● How to Replace Screening in a Metal Frame

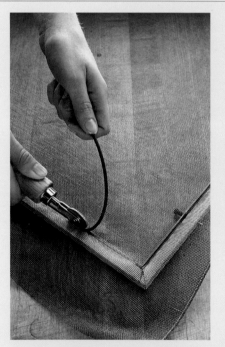

1 **Remove the screen** from the window and lay it on a flat work surface. Pry up the end of the spline cord with a small screwdriver, then pull out the rest of the spline by hand. Remove the old screening.

2 **Cut a new piece of screen** a few inches larger on all sides than the frame. Lay it over the frame opening and secure one edge by forcing the spline cord into the channel with a spline roller. Pull the screen taut and secure the remaining edges by rolling the spine into the groove. Trim off excess screening.

Variation: For wood frames, remove the wood trim piece to access and remove staples and the old screen. Fasten new screening to the frame using ¼" staples driven every 2". Pull the screen taut as you go.

Installing Replacement Windows

Having windows replaced by a professional outfitter is very expensive–$300 to $900 a window depending on size and construction—but sometimes it just has to be done. If you're an ambitious DIYer, however, you can save thousands of dollars by doing the work yourself. In addition to saving on labor costs, you can comparison shop for the best deal on windows (most installers require that you buy the windows through them). If you're replacing windows yourself you have two options: buy replacement sashes that fit into your existing window frames, or tear out the old window frames and do a complete unit replacement.

Replacement window sashes are easy to install as long as you have measured and ordered correctly. (Many stores offer guidance or even on-site services to ensure proper measurement.) You simply pop out the old window sashes, stops, and sash cord (left photo). Then, install new window mechanisms and sashes (right photo), weatherstripping, and trim.

Replacement windows for remodeling come prehung in window frames that are installed in framed window openings, usually with nailing flanges. The siding must be cut back to make clearance for the flashing (left photo) and nailing flanges (right photo). If you plan correctly, the removed siding area will be filled with exterior trim called brickmolding.

Exterior Improvements

In this chapter, we'll cover basic exterior home fix-ups from top to bottom. This sequence isn't just a tidy way to organize a chapter; it's also the best approach to tackling exterior repairs. The logic here is as right as rain: When water hits your roof, it runs down the shingles toward the gutters. Any holes it finds along the way may lead the water into the attic or, worse, the living spaces below (time to repaint the ceiling). If the gutters are dirty, leaky, or sagging, the water drips or overflows down onto the siding and trim, bringing the dirt and rotting leaves along with it and messing up the walls. That's why it's wise to make repairs from the top down.

Once you've taken care of the most pressing practical matters, you can focus your attention on aesthetic improvements, like washing the siding and touching-up or repainting the trim. And don't ignore the "floors" of your outdoor home—the driveway, patios and stoops, decks, and the always-scrutinized walkway leading up to the front door. Simple cosmetic upgrades are the secrets to erasing years of use and weathering without blowing your budget.

Roof Repairs

If you're like most people, you pay absolutely no attention to your roof until one fateful day when you make the heart-sinking discovery that you have a leak. Don't worry; a single leak may not be that bad. Chances are the problem lies in one localized area and you can fix it using ordinary tools and materials. But fix it you must. Leaving it for future owners to discover could lead to litigation, and you'd be crazy to ignore a leak if you're staying in the home (water is the enemy of house structures). Be aware that home inspectors, unlike owners, pay very close attention to roofs when writing their reports. It behooves sellers to examine their own roof and make necessary repairs before the official inspection. For new owners, the inspector's report can be a handy source for identifying and locating shortcomings in the roofing systems.

Often the hardest part of repairing a roof is finding the source of a leak. This is because water that gets through the roofing material can travel great distances along the building paper, roof decking, or even the rafters before it drops onto the top of your ceiling or runs down the inside of a wall. So unless your roof's been hit by a meteorite, you can assume the breech in the roofing is not directly above the drip in your ceiling. To find the source of the leak, go into the attic with a flashlight and examine the roof deck and rafters above and around the vicinity of the leak. Look for moisture or discoloration of the wood indicating the water's path. On a dry day, when you're ready to make repairs, drive a nail up through the roof from underneath so you can find the leak when you're on the rooftop.

Common areas for leaks include cracked, loose, or missing shingles; flashing (pieces of metal sheeting along roof junctures); penetrations, such as plumbing vents, air vents, and chimneys; and skylights. It's a good idea to check all of these while you're up on the roof, even if they don't seem to be leaking...yet.

Preventing Roof Damage

When it comes to keeping your roof in good shape, an ounce of prevention can save thousands of dollars in repairs. First make sure your roof is properly ventilated—that air coming in through soffit vents flows unobstructed out ridge or gable end vents. If you live in a region where snowfall is common, the attic space should be properly insulated so that snow does not melt and then freeze, creating damaging ice dams. A twice-yearly cleaning and inspection of your gutters and downspouts will go a long way toward preventing leaks.

Problems with your roof system show up from any angle and send a clear message. And if you can see a problem from the exterior, the chances are good it is causing damage to the interior as well.

Repair or Re-roof?

There's no question that a roof's condition is a major consideration in any home sale or purchase. But that doesn't mean you're guaranteed to make a profit or even to break even by investing in a new roof prior to selling your home. Standard asphalt shingle roofing, found on the vast majority of American homes, has an estimated lifespan of about 15 to 25 years (the actual number is less than 10 years).

If your roof is in good shape generally and is less than 15 years old, it's probably wiser to make a few minor repairs in worn areas than to replace the roof. The age of a roof is typically a disclosure item, and an old roof usually becomes a bargaining point for buyers. New roofing that's installed as a single layer—that is, after the old shingles have been removed first—is considered more desirable and more valuable than re-roof jobs that have one or two layers of old shingles below.

If only a few of your shingles look like this, you can probably get by with some spot repairs to your roof. If more than 1 in 10 are in rough shape, remove and replace all the shingles.

Making Spot Repairs

Roof leaks can come from any number of minor flaws: misplaced nails, inadequate sealant, even holes left behind when you took down an old basketball hoop (a recommended task for all sellers). These call for an all-in-one, instant repair kit: a tube of asphalt plastic roofing cement. Black, gooey, and unavoidably messy, this stuff sticks to anything. Squirt it into holes and spread it out a little along the edges with a stick or putty knife, and call it good.

But as good as it is, just as no amount of regular caulk can hide the fact that you cut your crown molding way too short, roofing cement should not be used in place of permanent building materials, such as flashing. It also doesn't work that well when applied over the top of old, cracked roofing cement, no matter how much you gob on. It is especially ineffective on lighter colored roofs, where the black color stands out.

If spot repairs made with roofing cement will be visible from the ground, embed mineral granules swept up from the surface of surrounding shingles into the wet cement to help it blend in. Use a light touch and do not harvest too many granules from the same shingle.

Replacing Shingles

Asphalt shingles that are cupped or curled up at the edges can be glued down flat with roofing cement—for a while at least. Roofing cement also can be used to seal minor cracks and fill in dents or small holes. But if a shingle is badly damaged or is missing at least part of a tab, it should be replaced. Replacing one or even a few shingles is a simple job. The most challenging part may be finding replacement pieces that match your old shingles.

Wood shingles call for replacement when they're badly split or are missing altogether. Here again, look to match the type of wood used for the original shingles.

In either case, the first objective is to do no other harm to the roof. Be careful in making replacements and, if you're not sure of yourself, call a roofing contractor.

Lastly, no matter who does the repairs, safety should be a primary concern. It's wise to always use some sort of fall-arrest system, such as a leash tethered to the chimney or a full harness. Use non-slip work boots, a sturdy ladder with a roof brace, and don't work on a wet roof.

Choosing Quality Shingles

Always replace damaged wood shingles with high-quality pieces that will last as long as the rest of the roof. Look for shingles rated Grade No. 1 to ensure they are free of defects. The best wood for shingles—replacement or original—is Western Red Cedar (but if your roof is made with another wood, look to match it). Lastly, ensure the integrity of your repair by asking if the shingles were treated. If they weren't, saturate the new shingles with a preservative and water repellant before installing.

● How to Replace Wood Shingles

1 **Split damaged wood shingles** with a chisel to remove them. Saw off the old nails as flush as possible with a hacksaw. Trim the replacement shingles to width, so they offset the seams below by at least 1½" while providing a ¼" gap between all adjacent shingles.

2 **Install the replacement shingles with nails,** maintaining the ¼" gap on both sides. Trim to length as necessary to position the shingles. Install them working from the bottom up. Nail each shingle with two 4d galvanized nails. Seal under exposed nail heads with urethane caulk before driving them home.

Aging Wood Shingles

To "age" new wood shingles, brush on a solution of 1 pound of baking soda dissolved in 1 gallon of water. Place the wet shingles in direct sunlight for four to five hours, then rinse them thoroughly and let them dry. Repeat the process as needed to match the coloring on the old shingles.

How to Replace Damaged Asphalt Shingles

1 **Break the seal under the ends of the tabs** using a putty knife or trowel. Remove the damaged shingle or shingles by pulling down on it. Insert a flat pry bay under the shingle overhanging the repair area to pry out roofing nails. Be careful not to damage the surrounding shingles. If you're replacing more than one row of shingles, remove them from the top down.

2 **Patch any damaged building paper** with new paper. Insert the new shingle so it lines up with adjacent shingles. Lift up the tabs of the shingle above and nail the new shingle with 1" roofing nails driven along the nailing line. Start from the bottom of the repair area if you are replacing more than one row of shingles.

3 **Apply roofing cement** to the backside of the last shingle to fill in the repair area and insert it underneath the tabs of the overhanging shingle above.

Ridge Caps

An area of the roof that tends to wear more quickly than other places is the row of cap shingles along the ridge. These shingles are especially susceptible to wind damage, falling tree limbs, and people walking on them (which you should never do). The caps are fastened with a nail on each side above the exposure line so that they are hidden by the next cap shingle. To replace one or more bad cap shingles, remove the damaged pieces with a flat pry bar and pull all of the nails. Replace any missing or damaged building paper. Follow the steps on this page to complete the repair.

Ridge Cap Economy

You can save a small bit of money by making your own ridge cap shingles rather than buying actual ridge caps. Simply cut one of the tabs off a three-tab roofing shingle, tapering the back end of the shingle to form a shape roughly similar to a home plate in baseball. The shingle is set in place with the wider end at the front or leading edge, and the narrower end slid under the previous cap shingle.

Ridge Caps for Wood Roofs

The easiest way to replace a missing or badly damaged ridge cap on a wood-shingle roof is with a preassembled cap unit. These are available in standard lengths of 16" and 18". Remove the damaged pieces and old nails, then replace any damaged or missing building paper. Install the new cap with galvanized shingle nails, using the original installation as a guide.

● How to Repair a Ridge Cap

1 **Fasten replacement caps in place** with 1¼" roofing nails. Use one nail along each side, about 1" in from the side edges.

2 **Slip the final cap shingle** under the existing cap shingle. Set it in place with roofing cement underneath and nail it down. Cover the nailheads with roofing cement.

Repairing Flashing

Roof flashing is made of galvanized metal, aluminum, or (rarely) copper. It usually outlasts the actual roofing material, but it can corrode through or create openings where sealant has failed.

Plumbing vents coming up through the roof should be flashed with a special collar that has a broad, metal base and a neoprene boot that seals tightly around the pipe. This is commonly called vent-pipe flashing or jack flashing. The inner portion of the rubber boot can be peeled away to accommodate larger pipes, for one-size-fits-all application.

Flashing around chimneys and other less uniform structures are created by overlapping layers of metal —with the higher layers overlapping those lower on the roof to create proper drainage. The flashing is nailed down and sealed with roofing cement liberally applied along seams, inside and outside edges, and over nail heads (before shingles are reinstalled over the flashing). To install new vent-pipe flashing, remove the shingles above the pipe, then apply a bead of roofing cement under the flashing base and set it into place. Nail the base flange along its top edge. Install new shingles to cover the top half of the base, trimming the shingles as needed so they lie flat around the base of the boot.

Valley flashing is a continuous channel that runs between two intersecting roof planes. You can temporarily patch holes in valley flashing with a piece of the same type of flashing material (don't use dissimilar metals, which promotes corrosion). Patching flashing isn't ideal, but a careful repair job should get you by until the roofing needs to be replaced.

● How to Replace Vent Pipe Flashing

Install vent-pipe flashing by removing the shingles above the pipe and overlapping shingles below. Apply a bead of roofing cement under the flashing base and nail along the base flange. Finish with shingles installed over the top of the flashing.

● How to Repair Valley Flashing

Repair a hole in valley flashing by cutting a patch wide enough to lap under shingles on both sides. Cut a slit in the valley, above the hole, and tuck the pointed end of a patch into it. Seal all joints and seams with a heavy bead of roofing cement.

Gutters

Everyone knows that gutters are there to catch rainwater and snowmelt coming down the roof and channel it to downspouts to carry it away from the house. What you might not know is why gutters are so important. Without them, all of that excess water would drop right down to the foot of the exterior walls, making a mess of the siding and saturating the soil around the foundation. Eventually, some of that water would likely end up inside your crawlspace or basement, leading to efflorescence (see page 135), mold, and other moisture problems.

In addition to their critical role in keeping your basement dry, gutters are highly visible elements that can seriously detract from your home's appearance when they're weather-beaten and sagging.

The two main problems affecting gutters are sagging and leaks. Sagging not only looks bad, but it interferes with proper gutter function—gutters need to slope toward downspouts at a rate of 1/16 inch per foot, or more, for proper drainage. Fixing sags usually means replacing one or more gutter hangers. We've shown a repair to the most common spike-and-ferrule type here, but you may have a different style. The idea is the same though: Replace the worn or damaged hanger as soon as the gutter begins to sag. Refastening the hangers will get a droopy

gutter back in line, and a good cleaning can make old parts look like new

Leaks are a bigger problem. Over time, every gutter will leak, so we've shown a few ways to deal with the situation. If your gutters have many leaks and have already been repaired in several places, it may be time for new gutters.

Low-Value Gutter Guards

Keeping gutters clean is crucial to maintaining your roof's drainage system, but it's a messy, unpleasant chore that needs to be done three to four times a year. Manufacturers have responded with a range of solutions that claim to eliminate the need for cleaning. The two basic styles are screens or shields that block the top of the gutter, or foam that sits inside and lets water through but blocks debris. The solutions are not cheap, ranging from $1 to $5 per linear foot. Unfortunately, it's generally not money well spent. Smaller plant waste finds its way in, and these solutions themselves often set up conditions for mold growth. Sadly, the best solution remains a good thorough cleaning a few times each year.

How to Fix Sagging Gutters

1 **Remove a loose gutter spike** with a pry bar, using a wood block to prevent crushing the gutter as you pry. A mason's string tied to follow the original slope line lets you know how far up you need to move the gutter.

2 **A long gutter screw** goes deeper than a spike so it can grab the framing behind the fascia trim. Gutter screws are made to fit through standard hanger ferrules.

How to Fix a Leaking Gutter

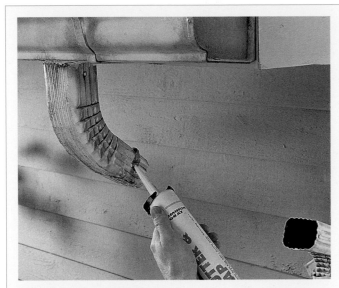

1 **Scrub the area clean** with a wire brush, removing dirt and rust. Apply an even layer of roofing cement about ⅛" thick over the damaged area and a few inches past it on every side.

2 **Cut and bend a piece of flashing** to fit as a patch. Bed it In the roofing cement. Coat the patch with a thin layer of roofing cement, feathered at the ends to prevent damming. To prevent corrosion, the patch should match the metal of the gutter. Patch vinyl gutters with aluminum or steel and bond the patch with silicone caulk instead of roofing cement.

Seal leaks at joints between gutter sections by cleaning the area thoroughly and applying new self-leveling gutter seam sealant with a caulk gun.

Instant Hole Repair

If you're really pressed for time (or patience), you can temporarily patch a hole with gutter repair tape. Some versions cover the hole from the inside of the channel, while others are large patches that you stick over the entire outer profile of the channel. Inner versions are less visible from the ground. Outer patches can be painted and are better for hiding ugly rusted areas.

Siding & Trim

Sprucing up the siding and trim on your house doesn't have to be a monstrous job, but it goes a long way toward creating a positive first impression. Often a good cleaning and a little touch-up paint can get the exterior in selling shape or, if you're a new owner, will buy you some time before the inevitable undertaking of a complete house repainting. Individual siding and trim boards that have rotted or are otherwise badly deteriorated can be replaced, and weathered brick can be renewed with tuck-pointing. If you're hoping for a more dramatic renewal or want to add some personality to a drab facade, repainting the trim for contrast is a good quick-fix option.

Pressure Washing Your House

Like everything outdoors, houses get dirty. And when appearance counts, a thorough washing can have just as big of an impact as a fresh coat of paint. Of course, you can always wash a house the old-fashioned way—with a scrub brush, a sponge, and a garden hose. But this seems about as efficient as cutting your lawn with scissors. For a quick fix, a pressure washer is the right tool for the job (provided you use the tool correctly).

Pressure washers, also called power washers, are commonly available for rent at about $50 to $75 a day. If you need one for more than a day's work, it makes sense to buy a simple electric model, starting at around $120. For most cleaning jobs around the house and yard, a washer with 1300 to 1600 psi (pounds per square inch) of pressure is all you need. Most washers include a siphon tube or a reservoir for automatically mixing liquid detergent into the spray. This is a handy feature to have for washing a dirty house.

Before you get started, read all instructions and safety precautions that come with your washer, or be sure to ask the pro at the rental center about adjusting the spray pressure and operating the machine safely. Always wear safety goggles when spraying, and never direct the spray toward yourself or anyone else. A high-pressure spray can easily injure skin, or virtually any other material at close range.

Damaged or worn siding is a common enough sight, but that doesn't mean you have to let it infect your house. The difficulty of making repairs depends largely on what kind of siding you have, but in every case it is worth the time and effort.

A few more words of warning: Don't spray near electrical cables, power lines, or any electrical devices such as fixtures, receptacles, and air conditioning units. Avoid spraying doors and windows to prevent water damage or destroying the seals around glazing. Pressure washers are generally considered safe for most types of vinyl, aluminum, and painted wood siding. However, they are too aggressive to be used on stucco, hardboard siding (such as Masonite®), old masonry, or brick with a sand or slurry finish.

Always direct the spray at a downward angle to the siding. Spraying upward can force water underneath the siding joints and into the wall cavity. The sprayer should never be held closer than 13 inches to the siding.

To give your house a much-deserved bath, start by covering bushes and other plantings in the area with plastic, to protect them from the cleaning detergent. You should use a general-purpose detergent that doesn't contain bleach, which can burn foliage. Hose down any plantings that can't be covered, and keep them wet throughout the process.

In addition to the pressure setting, the cleaning power of the spray can be adjusted in two ways: by selecting a different spray pattern and by altering the distance between the sprayer and the wall. A wider pattern and greater spray distance produces a gentler spray. Focusing the pattern and moving closer increases the water's impact. In general, you want to find the lowest impact settings that still produce effective cleaning.

Optimizing Rental Time

Because most rental centers charge by the full day, it only makes sense to use a rental pressure washer for a full day whenever possible. If you finish washing the house, use the pressure washer to bring a fresh new look to driveways, sidewalks, walks, decks, and patios.

How to Pressure Wash Your House

1 **Set up the pressure washer,** adjusting the settings to the manufacturer's recommendations (the lowest pressure is a good place to start). Use an approved detergent and hook the washer up to your water source.

2 **Wash the siding** with a non-bleach detergent solution, starting at the bottom. Maintain a downward angle with the water spray. Use caution when working on ladders or scaffolding (scaffolding is a much safer choice).

3 **Let the detergent sit** for the recommended time. Rinse the siding from the top down. Maintain as little impact as necessary to remove dirt and detergent without damaging the surfaces. Continue on to the next section as each part is washed and rinsed. Rinse the entire wall from the top down after it has been completely washed.

Quick & Inexpensive Fix for Rotted Siding & Trim

When a nice-looking (and probably expensive) piece of siding or trim seems fatally flawed by localized rot and decay, you'd be understandably loathe to replace the whole piece. And cutting out the damaged section is rarely an easy job. Here's a permanent repair that lets you keep your saw on the shelf and your money (most of it, at least) in your wallet.

1 Remove all rotted and decayed wood with a chisel, then brush or vacuum the area clean. Punch several holes in the damaged area, using an awl. Be sure the area is dry before proceeding.

2 Apply a wood-hardening resin to the repair area with a disposable brush, adding several coats as needed. Let dry.

3 Force a strong, two-part polymerized wood filler or epoxy deep into the cavity and smooth the surface with a putty knife. Sand smooth after the filler dries. Prime and paint immediately.

Variation: If you are repairing a wood part with a more complicated profile, you can use a Surform plane to shape the repair material after it dries.

Siding

Often the easiest fix for a piece of siding or trim with some isolated damage is to replace the entire piece instead of attempting to make a small patch. There are, however, some general exceptions to full-board replacement. If the damaged piece is very long, you might have a hard time finding a replacement or, when you do, it may be expensive. In this case, install a shorter replacement that's long enough to span at least a few stud spaces. Make sure the joints of the patch will blend with the joint offsets on the surrounding siding, as you would for long trim boards. Another exception involves cases where rotted or damaged wood millwork pieces are difficult to replace, such as exterior window sills or ornamental trim. For these, the best quick fix is to carve out the bad wood and rebuild the area with wood filler.

Repairing & Patching Wood Siding

To replace a piece of horizontal lap siding, first determine how the siding is installed. Most wood horizontal siding is fastened to the wall framing and/or sheathing with nails. Find out how the boards are joined to one another. Some types fit together with tongue-and-groove joints, some have rabbeted back edges that fit over the top edges of the siding below, and some have flat back sides and are simply lapped over the preceding course. You want to know which type you have so you don't ruin the joint edges when removing the damaged piece.

Use the technique shown to pop siding nails and pull them out. Remove all nails along the bottom edge, then repeat the technique to remove the nails along the bottom edge of the piece above the damaged board. Slide out the damaged piece. Replace any building paper that is missing or damaged.

Cut the new siding piece to length. Prime both sides and all edges of the board with exterior primer (this is important to prevent warpage). Slip the new piece up under the siding above so the exposed width of the face matches the other pieces. Fasten the new piece using the same nail holes, but use siding nails that are about 1" longer than the originals. Paint the new board to match.

Repairing lap siding, whether wood, vinyl, or metal, is mostly a matter of finding similar patch materials and working it into the wall as seamlessly as possible.

Some types of siding are nailed at the top and bottom edges, with each nail penetrating two pieces at once. Remove the nails by prying up the edge slightly, then hammering the board to pop the nail heads. This is especially useful for pulling the nails on the good pieces.

Replacing Wood Shingle Siding

Wood shingles are installed just like wood roofing shingles, with two nails driven above the butt edge of the shingles above. Fasten replacement pieces with two nails only, and seal the nail heads with caulk. See page 104 for the basic removal and replacement steps.

Repairing & Replacing Vinyl Siding

Replacing vinyl siding requires a special hand tool, called a zip tool, to unlock the channel along the bottom edge of the siding. Unlock the channel on the damaged piece and the piece above, then pry up the piece above slightly to access the nails securing the damaged piece. Pull the nails and remove the damaged piece. Cut the replacement piece to the same length, following the manufacturer's directions, and fasten it in the same fashion as the old piece.

Repairing Brick Siding

Barring structural problems, the most common repair for brick wall veneer (technically a form of siding) and other brickwork is tuck-pointing—the process of filling deteriorated mortar joints with fresh mortar. This takes a little practice and patience but is an easy and inexpensive job that greatly improves the appearance of brick structures. *Note: Large cracks and apparent shifting of brickwork indicate structural failure, for which tuck-pointing is not an effective or appropriate repair. Consult a mason in such cases.*

    One tricky part of tuck-pointing is matching the new mortar to the old. If the old mortar is tinted—that is, not standard gray—borrow a set of mortar tint samples from a masonry supplier, and follow the mixing directions for the color that is the best match. For most tuck-pointing repairs, use type N mortar mixed with acrylic or latex concrete fortifier for strength and improved adhesion.

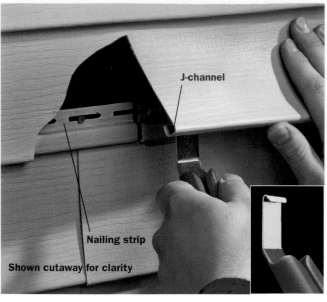

Use a zip tool (inset) to unlock the channels on vinyl siding. Install the replacement piece following the manufacturer's specifications and nailing techniques.

On the Flip Side

If your siding has the same profile on both sides, and the damage to the face is merely cosmetic, you might be able to flip it over and install it with the backside out, saving you the cost of a replacement board. After you flip, fill the old nail holes with non-shrinking exterior vinyl spackle and paint the board to match. Only you will be the wiser.

● How to Tuck-Point Brick Siding

1 **Clean out loose and crumbling mortar** with a raking tool (inset). Clear debris and moisten the joints with water. Tuck-point the cleaned mortar joints with a tuck-pointer and mortar hawk. Apply mortar in ¼"-thick layers, letting it dry for 30 minutes between applications.

2 **Tuck point the vertical joints** using the same technique. When all joints are filled, smooth them with a jointing tool to match the old mortar joints. Let the mortar dry, then brush off excess with stiff bristle brush.

Stucco

Although stucco siding is very durable, it can be damaged, and over time it can crumble or crack. The directions given below work well for patching small areas less than two square feet. For more extensive damage, the repair is done in layers.

Fill thin cracks in stucco walls with a sanded acyrlic stucco caulk. Overfill the crack with caulk and feather until it's flush with the stucco. Allow the caulk to set, then paint it to match the stucco. Masonry caulk stays semiflexible, preventing further cracking.

Premixed stucco patch works well for small holes, cracks, or surface defects. Repairs to large damaged areas often require the application of multiple layers of base coat stucco and a finish coat stucco. Matching the stucco texture may require some practice.

Painting Stucco

One reason homebuilders install stucco siding is that it does not require painting. If a color is desired, it is created by tinting the stucco mixture before application. But many stucco houses do get painted, and once they have been under the brush there is no going back. If your painted stucco needs refreshing, select a paint that is formulated for stucco and masonry. These alkali-resistant paints run about $25 per gallon and are best applied with a paint roller that has a ¾- to 1" nap.

● How to Patch Small Areas

1 Remove loose material from the repair area using a wire brush. Use the brush to clean away rust from any exposed metal lath, then apply a coat of metal primer to the lath.

2 Apply premixed stucco patch compound to the repair area using a putty knife or trowel, slightly overfilling the hole.

3 Smooth the repair with a putty knife or trowel, feathering the edges to blend into the surrounding surface. Use a whisk broom or trowel to duplicate the original texture. Let the patch dry for several days, then touch it up with masonry paint.

Touching-up Exterior Paint

New paint has the same transformative effect on the outside of a house as it does for interior spaces. And yet, no one expects exterior walls to look as pristine as those in a bedroom or kitchen. If the siding is clean and the paint isn't peeling or flaking off in large areas—it's important that the materials are well protected—why repaint? Instead, take care of limited problem areas with touch-ups and move on to your next project. If the house could use some perking up to add definition and curb appeal, consider repainting the trim with a contrasting but complementary color.

Touch-ups are most successful when the new paint exactly matches the old. The walls and trim must also be perfectly clean before you add new paint. If you don't have reserves of the original paint, take a sample to a paint store or home center. Most have electronic color-matching equipment that can find the precise blend in a matter of seconds. Once the new paint is mixed, dab a little right onto your sample and let it dry. This will show you how close the match is. If the color looks off, even just a little, have the salesperson try again until the match is perfect.

To touch up areas where the old paint is peeling or bubbled, remove all loose paint. *Note: Take all necessary precautions if you suspect the old paint might contain lead.*

If you're repainting trim, take the time to remove any failed caulking along trim joints and where window and door casings meet the siding. Don't apply caulk underneath window casings or under the lap joints on horizontal siding—these areas need slight air gaps to help the wall breathe.

Prime any bare wood areas with an acrylic or oil-base primer that is compatible with your finish paint. When the primer has dried, apply one or two finish coats as needed to cover the primer.

Small sections of blistered or failing paint can be touched up easily to make a dramatic improvement in the appearance of your house, and to protect the siding and trim.

Thrifty Painting

When touching up exterior paint, you may be tempted to buy a quart or even a gallon. But the more economical solution is a sample jar. Available at large home centers and many paint stores, these small (usually 8 oz.) jars contain the perfect amount of paint for touch-ups, and the small price matches the tiny size.

Painting the trim and gutters with a nicely contrasting color can liven-up the whole house—without all the trouble and expense of a comprehensive paint job.

Prepping Exterior Surfaces

Scraping off old, loose paint for touch-ups is a must before adding primer and the topcoat. Feather in rough areas by sanding all scraped spots with 110-grit sandpaper before laying on paint.

Surface Preparation

Whether you are touching up a small section of siding, painting a whole wall, or painting your entire house, sanding and scraping the old paint is the only way to get a smooth, professional-looking finish. At a minimum you should either pressure-wash the siding or hand-scrub it with a stiff bristle brush and detergent, rinsing completely when you're done. Both of these processes will dislodge some flaking paint if it is present. Scraping is also advised if the old paint is failing. Sanding can be done to feather out scraped areas where paint has been removed, and to resurface the siding down to bare wood.

Sanded to bare wood

Scraped and spot-sanded

Pressure-washed only

Use a power sander such as this siding sander for best results when addressing failing paint. Even with a siding sander, removing old paint from an entire house is a laborious job.

Revive wood shingles by re-staining them with wood stain. If your house was treated with penetrating stain that does not form a film layer, you don't need to do any preparation beyond washing.

Drives & Walkways

Concrete and asphalt surfaces are prime candidates for quick fixes. Although they may look weathered and shabby on top, they seldom need to be completely replaced. This is especially true of concrete. So if your outdoor surfaces are starting to show their age, treat them to a facelift so they can at least look young again.

Most problems in driveways, walks, and steps are caused by either movement in the underlying surface or failure of improperly laid or cured concrete. The results are usually cracks, holes or, in some cases, a general degradation of large patches across the surface of the concrete. Minor problems are easily fixed with spot treatments. However, in highly visible locations even spot treatments may be unacceptable. To completely cover up large damaged areas, or telltale signs of repair, consider a complete resurfacing. You can use any of a number of resurfacing kits for a thin top coat over an otherwise stable surface, or choose to use a stiffer mix for more degraded surfaces.

Regardless of what repair is called for, fixing concrete problems is more an investment of time and effort than of money. And the results often dramatically affect your home's curb appeal.

A little unevenness in a curved pathway can be charming, but major sinking and heaving, along with other concrete problems, calls for some attention. Here, the sunken concrete sections can simply be pried up with a lever (such as a 2 × 4) so gravel backfill can be added to bring them to level.

Easy, Low-Cost Crack Solutions

At around $3 a tube, flexible urethane concrete repair caulk is a bargain and an easy solution to smaller (up to ¼"-wide) cracks. Just clean out the crack with a bristle brush and fill with the self-leveling, quick-drying caulk. Don't let it spread onto the areas outside the crack because it could peel. For larger cracks, chisel at a downward angle to create a "key" and remove debris. Fill the crack with sand or caulk backer rod to within ½" of the surface, and then fill with premixed concrete filler containing acrylic fortifier. Level the surface with a trowel, cover with plastic, and let cure for a week.

How to Patch Small Holes

1 **Cut margins around the damage** using a drill equipped with a masonry-grinding disc, a dremel tool with grinding attachment, or hammer and chisel (always use gloves and safety glasses). Bevel cuts at an angle away from the center of the hole. Remove loose debris.

2 **If the patch repair compound** you're using requires it, brush a coating of bonding agent onto the damaged area to create a bonding surface for the compound. Wait for the agent to become tacky (no more than 30 minutes) and proceed to the next step. (Many pre-mixed patching compounds don't require this step.)

3 **Fill in the hole** with patching compound (mix first, according to manufacturer's directions, if you're using a two-part epoxy compound). Use a trowel to level the top surface and feather into the surrounding areas. Let dry for the time recommended by the manufacturer.

How to Patch Large Holes

1 **Mark straight cutting lines** around the damaged area and cut with circular saw equipped with a masonry blade. Set the saw angle to cut at 15 degrees or more away from the center of the damaged area. *Tip: Set the foot of the saw on a scrap piece to protect from the concrete. Chisel out lose pieces within the damaged area, and brush clean.*

2 **Use patching compound** recommended for large areas, or a small batch of sand-mix concrete with acrylic fortifier. Fill the hole with the mix so that the top sits slightly higher than the surrounding areas. When filled, use a float to level the patch, cover with plastic, and let cure undisturbed for one week (or according to patch compound manufacturer's instructions).

How to Resurface Concrete—Horizontal

1 **Clean the slab** with a commercial concrete cleaner, followed by pressure washing (see pages 110 to 111 for more information on pressure washing). Use high pressure in a fan spray. Let the slab dry and repair cracks and deep holes. *Note: You can use the resurfacer to fill shallow holes and dips, mixing it drier than normal. Smooth all repairs level with the surrounding surface and let them dry as directed.*

2 **Soak the slab** with water, then squeegee dry. For large flat surfaces, apply thin resurfacer with a squeegee or roller. Let the resurfacer cure as directed. For smaller areas in bad condition, trowel on a stiffer mixture. Apply multiple layers if necessary, waiting 15 or 20 minutes between applications. To create a non-slip surface texture, pull a push broom over the surface after it has set for about ten minutes.

How to Resurface Concrete—Vertical

1 **Thoroughly clean out the damaged area,** removing loose and crumbling debris. Powerwash if possible, and use a concrete cleanser to prepare the surface.

2 **Trowel on hydraulic or quick-setting cement,** or quick-drying stiff resurfacer specifically meant for vertical surfaces. Use a stiff brush to feather the patch into the surrounding areas. Use long, continuous strokes for a broomed finish, or short strokes for a mottled texture.

Renewing Asphalt Surfaces

Asphalt driveways and surfaces are subjected to a great deal of abuse, both from the elements and from the traffic they support. That's why it's a good idea to apply a general resurfacing sealant over an asphalt driveway once a year in areas where temperatures reach freezing. Along the way, though, it's a good idea to treat holes and cracks as quickly as possible; they can serve as conduits for water and ice that can quickly undermine and compromise the entire surface.

Basic asphalt repairs are a cinch. Repair cracks with a self-leveling filler that contains a lot of rubber. Buy a name-brand product—in a tube ($3.50), a gallon jug with caulking nozzle, or a gallon pail of trowelable filler for deeper cracks (both $10).The right material for patching holes depends on the size of the hole. For smaller holes, use an asphalt patching mix (about $6). Larger holes call for a trowel-grade filler or "cold patch" asphalt repair compound (around $11 for a gallon). Either way, the hole needs to be clean and free of loose debris. Use a wire brush or screwdriver on a small hole, and vacuum it out. Larger holes require a chisel, to square out the hole, creating suitable edges that won't erode.

A typical asphalt (blacktop) driveway is formed by pouring and compressing a layer of hot asphalt over a compressed gravel subbase. Repairs are usually done with product that's applied cold.

The Value of Resurfacing

Regularly resurfacing and sealing an asphalt driveway can save you bundles in the long run, not only on crack and hole repairs, but in additional years before the driveway requires repaving. The process is easy. Thoroughly clean the driveway (a pressure washer is best), and then use a squeegee or pushbroom to spread the resurfacing/sealant evenly across the driveway. A 5-gal. pail will cover about 350 sq. ft. and runs about $30. The investment can easily save you hundreds in an extended driveway life.

● How to Repair Asphalt Damage

1 **Clean the hole** thoroughly and square the edges if the hole is deeper than ½". Fill with asphalt patching mix and tamp with a hand tamper or the butt of a 4 × 4 post. Add mix until the repair is flush with the surrounding surface.

2 **Cover the patch** with scrap plywood and weight the board down to help the repair to properly set.

Variation: Fill a crack by first cleaning out all dirt, debris, and plants. Cut the tip of the tube or gallon jug to suit the size of the crack. Fill the crack and smooth with a putty knife. Let the filler dry as directed before walking or driving over the crack.

Decks

When it's time to turn a critical eye to your deck, you'll likely face some common questions: Do I really have to refinish the weathered wood on my deck, or can I just paint it instead? What are the best improvements to make? What are buyers looking for?

The following are some suggestions to help you navigate those questions. If you live in an area where outdoor entertaining is a favorite pastime, an inviting outdoor space may be a strong selling point for buyers. In many areas and markets, however, decks usually aren't deal-breakers.

But as a general rule, a deck has to be in good shape or it might be seen as a huge liability by home buyers and inspectors. Plan on replacing any rotted posts, joists, or decking boards so the deck feels reassuringly solid underfoot. If the finish is shot, it's time to bite the bullet and recoat the whole deck. Cedar and redwood decks should be scrubbed with a cleaning solution to remove all dirt and flaking finish materials. You can also use a pressure washer if you're very careful not to overdo it and damage the wood. A brightening agent, such as oxalic acid or non-chlorine bleach, can help remove dark streaks and bring up the wood's natural coloring. As for the new finish, most pros use a semi-transparent stain, which provides some UV protection without hiding the wood grain. Solid stains (which look like paint) are better for covering up ugly or discolored wood. Don't use regular house paint on a deck; it can't stand up to foot traffic.

Everlasting Decks

If you've decided to add a small deck as part of making your home more appealing to potential buyers (surveys show that decks often return 100% of their cost at resale), choose modern wood substitutes. Recent advances in synthetic composites mean that wood decking alternatives look amazingly like real wood with none of the maintenance. Although competitive in price to real wood, these materials will last virtually forever and require no refinishing or upkeep—a big plus to potential buyers.

Refinishing a deck takes only a couple of days—one day for cleaning and one day for applying the stain or waterproofing sealer. The payback is a "like new" appearance.

Replace rotting structural members and deck boards as soon as you detect them to prevent further damage. Use wood stain to try and match the color so the new wood blends in with the old deck, and attach the replacement board with screws instead of nails.

Patios

If your brick paver, stone, or concrete patio has gone south on you, it probably only needs a good, long day of grunt labor to get it back into shape. Unfortunately, you'll be supplying the labor (at least these repairs are cheap). Sunken pavers and stones set in sand can be pried up individually or en masse to be brought up to level with new sand underneath. Mortared brick and stone with deteriorating mortar joints can be tuck-pointed with fresh mortar (see page 114).

Concrete may not be the most glamorous of patio surfaces, but if that's what you've got to work with, the best thing for it is a good, thorough cleaning. Whatever you do, don't paint it. Concrete paint generally doesn't wear well with the temperature changes and abuse of an outdoor setting. If your patio surface looks really bad, consider resurfacing it (see page 120). Or you can cover it with brick or pavers.

(see page 114)
(see page 120)

Low-cost Weed Control

Expansion joints in concrete, spaces between patio bricks, and the locking lines between pavers are all ideal locations for weeds to set up shop. But don't spend your money on a continual supply of chemical weed killers. Choose a cheap (and more environmentally friendly) solution: straight white vinegar is an effective, nontoxic alternative that can be used regularly. Or boil heavily salted water for a more lasting solution—a few doses poured slowly over cracks will keep the patio weed-free for months.

Patio's got a sinking feeling? Pull up the pavers or stones, add sand as needed below, then re-set the pieces.

Concrete cleaner removes all sorts of common stains, including oil, dirt, and mildew. Follow the manufacturer's directions for use and safety precautions. A power wash will help make the surface look as sharp as possible.

Landscaping

Whether you're fixing up your house to sell or you've just bought a diamond in the rough, the first step to improving your landscape is to observe your home and its environs from every perspective. The objective is to absorb the visual effect of your yard, to see it as a house hunter will see it. We're talking, of course, about curb appeal, which is pretty much what front yards are all about. Backyards are important for many other reasons, of course.

Though a focus on curb appeal makes sense for both sellers and new owners, their approaches to outdoor fix-ups are often quite different. Sellers are obviously thinking about the short term. They want improvements that offer instant gratification and very little, if any, initial maintenance. New homeowners should think more carefully about the long term. What can you do now to have the landscape you want, and not just this season, but next year and every year thereafter? This might mean planting for a lush future, with bulbs, annuals, and seedling trees (which are much cheaper than mature trees).

Regardless of your goals, the good news is, basic yard makeovers require more sweat than money, or more effort from your back than your green thumb.

Shear Worth

A good pair of pruning shears are an essential part of your outdoor toolbox. High-quality shears ensure you don't waste money replacing plants—badly made shears tear stems and open plants to a range of infections. And on the subject of plant health, wipe down shears and loppers with rubbing alcohol after each use to prevent transmitting disease from one plant to another.

From the viewpoints of prospective buyers and new homeowners alike, a neat and low-maintenance landscape is a look that's very hard to beat.

Taming Trees & Shrubs

Overgrown trees and shrubs can give any landscape a shabby appearance. A quick pruning of mature plantings not only tidies everything up, it also promotes healthy new growth and, when done properly, strengthens the plant. Plants and tree limbs that grow too close to the house can damage siding, roofing, and gutters and should be cut back so there's no risk of contact during high winds or heavy snow or ice buildup. Dead trees and plants should be removed entirely. You can cut down small trees by yourself, but big ones are best left to a professional tree service.

When it comes to pruning and trimming, all dead branches and limbs should be the first to go. With the ugly and unhealthy stuff removed, give the plants a trim for a neat but natural look. As a general rule, never prune more than one-third of a tree's healthy branches. With shrubs and other low plantings, you can decide how manicured their look should be, but follow the same one-third rule. When in doubt, ask a professional before making any significant cutbacks.

Landscaping exists to complement the lines and proportions of your house. It doesn't need to steal the show and it shouldn't completely hide your house behind unruly overgrowth. Front-yard plantings look best when they frame and accent the house (and often the front entry) while adding definition to the property.

Pruning Shrubs

Pruning unkempt shrubs is the definition of a quick fix: it's fast, it's easy, and it's absolutely free. All you need are hand tools and possibly a ladder. For most tree and plant species, it's best to prune during the dormant period, typically late winter to early spring. Again, you can decide how to thin and shape your plantings, but here are some general techniques to follow:

Prune shrubs and bushes by hand, using pruning shears or hedge clippers, depending on how thick the stems or branches are. To promote fuller growth, trim the ends of healthy branches just above the buds (or near the starting point of soft, new growth), cutting at a 45 degree angle. This helps to stimulate new bud growth below, while preventing elongated shoots.

To shape full shrubbery, use hedge clippers to square off or round over the plants, as desired. The trick is to start conservatively, trimming inward from the ends in small increments. Don't just guess at the finished length of the growths and start hacking away at this level. If you do, you might cut off more than you want (or more than is healthy for the plant). Cautious shaping is especially important if you're trying for consistent sizing among a grouping of similar plants.

Careful pruning instantly gives plantings a trimmed look while encouraging healthy future growth. It also keeps vegetation away from your roof and siding, where moisture damage can occur.

Pruning Trees

Because of their larger size and slower growth, trees can be a little more complicated to prune than shrubs and bushes. Excessive or uneven pruning can be harmful for a tree, so it's wise not to take on a major pruning unless you know what you're doing. Removing dead branches, small, unsightly suckers, and any limbs that are growing within a couple of feet of your house is a safer approach. You can remove suckers—thin offshoots from the base of the tree—with pruning shears or a pruning saw. Do the same with larger branches that you can easily handle with one hand, using a pruning saw or bow saw.

Large branches are removed one small section at a time. As for tools, a pruning saw with a long extension pole is usually the safest tool for trimming trees, letting you reach many branches from the ground or without getting too high on a ladder. You can also use a bow saw or a chain saw, of course. If you own a reciprocating saw, you can now buy pruning blades that work much like a bow saw without as much effort. Leave cuts exposed so the tree can heal itself. Don't seal the cut with paint, tar, or other type of sealant.

Chainsaw Alternative

Although many pros prune trees with a chainsaw, a homeowner is often better off using a cordless reciprocating saw. The reciprocating saw is every bit as efficient in cutting the smaller trees of most suburban landscapes, and it costs $10 to $20 less than a comparable power chainsaw. See below.

⬤ How to Prune a Tree

1 **Remove larger tree branches** in small sections, starting at the end of the branch. Keep each section to a manageable length, one that you can easily handle with one hand.

2 **Make a shallow undercut** about halfway into the branch from below, several inches from the joint where the branch meets the trunk. Finish the cut from above.

3 **Complete the job** by trimming off the branch stub so it's flush with the outside of the bark collar. Support the stub as it falls away so it won't strip bark from the trunk.

Taming Trees & Shrubs

The first step to felling a tree is to decide the best place for it to fall—called the felling path. The path should be a clear space that's at least twice as long as the tree is tall.

When you're ready for the takedown, start by cutting off all branches below head level. Make a notch cut one third of the way into the diameter of the trunk. Do not notch all the way to the trunk's center. Next, make a level felling cut about two inches above the base of the notch, leaving three inches of solid wood between the felling cut and the notch. This creates a hinge for the tree to pivot from.

Drive a log-splitting wedge into the felling cut, using a hand maul or sledge. Push the tree toward the felling path to initiate the fall, then hightail it down one of your retreat paths. Once the tree is down, cut off all of the limbs and branches, then cut the trunk into manageable segments.

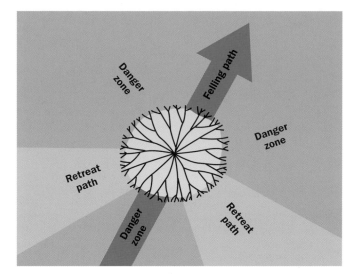

Good fellers plan their retreat. As shown, the predictably safe retreat paths angle away from the tree behind the felling path.

● How to Fell a Small to Medium Tree

1 Use a bow saw to remove limbs below head level. Start at the bottom of the branch, making a shallow up-cut. Then cut down from the top until the branch falls. Use a chain saw to make a notch cut one-third of the way through the tree. Do not cut to the center of the trunk.

2 Make a straight felling cut about 2" above the base of the notch cut, on the opposite side of the trunk. Leave a 3" hinge at the center.

3 Drive a wedge into the felling cut. Push the tree toward the felling path to start its fall, and move into a retreat path to avoid possible injury.

4 Standing on the opposite side of the trunk from the branch, remove each branch by cutting from the top of the saw, until the branch separates from the tree. Adopt a balanced stance, grasp the handles firmly with both hands, and be cautious with the saw.

Lawns

A turfgrass lawn is the predominant element in most home landscapes. As such, it carries the greatest burden of making the yard look good. Fortunately, most turfgrass is pretty darned resilient and will respond to a blitz of renewal measures if you have to green up a neglected lawn in a hurry. For areas that are too far gone, you can add new sod (if you're willing to spend some money) or reseed (if you have a little more time), or you can cut your losses and convert the really bad areas into planting beds, gravel edging, or mulch-and-shrub areas.

For new owners faced with renewing or maintaining an inherited lawn, it's a good idea to assess the condition, size, and shape of all the grassy areas and come up with a plan for the next growing season. If shrinking and re-shaping are part of your plan, it will be better to invest the time and money to make the cutbacks now, rather than spending one or more growing seasons keeping alive those areas slated for removal.

Revitalizing a tired, old lawn for a healthy, green future is a long, multi-stage process. The best approach involves holistic remedies to improve the health of the underlying soil, which in turn will promote strong grass plants that resist weeds and disease and ultimately reduce maintenance requirements. If you're a new owner hoping to nurse a sick lawn back to health, consult a local extension service for specific recommendations based on your type of grass and the local climate.

On the other hand, if you're selling your house, a quick green-and-go approach is more appropriate than a slow healing process. Your mantra should be something like this: Weed it, edge it, and water the heck out of it.

Money-Saving Mulcher

A mulching mower can improve the health of your lawn and save you time and money in eradicating weeds as well as reduce the amount of water your lawn consumes. But you don't need to run out and purchase a mulching mower. Just make sure the blades in your current mower are sharp, and run it without the bag, at a height that doesn't remove more than one-fifth of the grass blade (which usually means mowing twice a week). The clippings fall to the soil, suppress weeds, and conserve moisture.

As lifestyles change and water resources steadily dwindle, homeowners everywhere are reducing their "turf exposure" to areas they actually use or can easily manage. Limiting the grass is an especially good option if your new home's lawn comes without a sprinkler system.

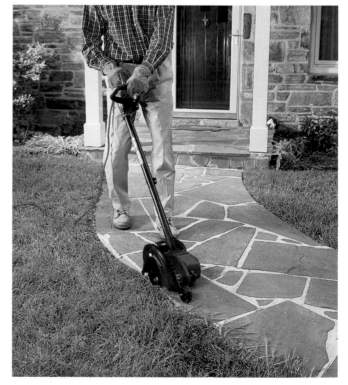

Edging a lawn is a quick fix that gives your yard a professionally manicured look. If you're just looking to spruce up for potential buyers, consider renting a power edger that'll do the job in minutes for about $30 a day. If you're a new homeowner who will likely be tending the lawn for years, you'll probably want to buy your own, for roughly three times that cost.

Patching Dead Lawn Spots

Dead patches ruin the impact of an otherwise green lawn. The fastest way to rid a lawn of brown patches is to fill them in with new sod. The slower—and much cheaper—method is to re-seed, using dry grass seed and soil or a lawn patch kit. Available at nurseries and garden centers, patch kits include seed mixed with a biodegradable mulch that keeps the seeds moist until they take root.

Here's the basic patching process: Dig out the dead grass and its roots, plus an inch or two of soil, using a shovel or hand spade, and cutting to the edges of healthy grass. Water the exposed area to wash away any pet urine or other materials that may have killed the grass in the first place. Amend the soil with a few inches of compost or leaf mold, mixing it into the soil with a shovel. Smooth and level the soil so it's even with the surrounding soil (if you're re-seeding) or is an inch or so below the surrounding soil (if you're laying sod).

Cover the soil with grass seed and mulch, as directed, or lay in a new plug of sod and lightly cover the edges of the patch with mulch or other organic matter to keep the edges moist. Water the patch as needed—typically at least once a day—until the patch is fully established.

Mulch Magic

Starting at around $15 per cubic yard (approximately 150 sq. ft. of ground cover at a little over 2" thick), wood-chip mulch is ideal for quick landscape makeovers. Use it as a general ground cover, to fill out planting beds, or to dress up bare rings around trees and shrubs. Tree service and landscape companies commonly deliver bulk orders of mulch in a variety of species and grinds (the number of grindings affects the look of the material). If you're able to load and haul mulch yourself, you might get some for free from your city or county maintenance departments.

Seeds in a lawn patch kit germinate in 4 to 6 days but take several weeks to achieve enough grass density to fill in the spot.

A sod patch yields immediate results. Like seed patches, sod must be watered regularly to help it take root and keep it alive after planting.

Creating Planting Beds

More than likely you have one or two shaded or sun-scorched spots in your lawn that are impossible to keep healthy. This is nature's way of telling you to give up the fight and throw down some ground cover. But first you have to do something with all the grass, weeds, and other unwanted growth. Just be careful if the area you're addressing surrounds a tree; consult with an arborist before disturbing the soil. Some types of trees have very shallow root systems that are easily damaged by light digging or even heavy foot traffic.

To turn those ugly areas into planting beds, all you have to do is dig up the grass and root layer and add topsoil and amendments to prepare for new plants or flowers. Start by marking the border of the bed with a garden hose, creating straight or curving lines as desired. Cut straight down along the border with a flat shovel or spade to form a clean edge. Then, dig out the grass and roots, removing about 3 inches of material to expose the pure soil underneath. You can do this with a good, sharp spade. It's a good idea to add border material along the edges of the bed to help prevent soil erosion and keep encroaching grass at bay. Black plastic edging is the cheapest and easiest border to install. Dig out the turf with a sharp spade and/or a mattock (a tool similar to a pick axe but with a broad, flat cutter on one end of the head). Once all the foliage is gone, cover the soil with landscape fabric. Lay down a two- to three-inch layer of rock or mulch as desired.

Landscape fabric and edging combine forces to control weeds, keep groundcover contained, and make mowing grass easier.

Soil Testing

Before choosing plants for your bed or buying fertilizer for your lawn or plants, you should invest in a soil test kit. A good kit can be had for $12 or less, and will help you save money by buying the right type and amount of fertilizer for your yard. It will also give you the info you need to shop more wisely for the plants that will do best in your beds.

Flowers for Fixer-Uppers

Whether they're found in planting beds, in pots on the front stoop, or in border strips along the driveway or front walkway, flowers are a great way to dress up a home for sale or to brighten your new home. Choose colorful annuals that complement the house and landscape. A blanket of wood-chip mulch covering the soil in the flowerbed adds a nice finishing touch and slows evaporation.

Landscape Lighting

Lighting can be a subtle yet effective way of attracting interested home buyers who decide to take a peek at your house after dark. It's also a nice way for new owners to send the message to neighbors that the house is now under the care of proud new residents.

Low-voltage landscape lights come in a huge range of styles and system configurations, but the easiest and cheapest fixtures to install are freestanding solar lights that require no digging, wiring, or exterior power supply (except, of course, the sun). All you have to do is spike them into the ground and let the sun take it from there. Position the lights wherever you want to highlight trees and other landscape features, brighten your home's facade, or create a welcoming path of light leading visitors to your front door.

If your house does not have a motion-detector security light near every entrance, install them. A floodlight or two directed out into the yard comes in handy for those late-night croquet matches, and a light that illuminates your house number so it can be read from the street is always a good idea.

Help your house sell itself at night with spotlights or floodlights shining up from the ground onto nice architectural features or your house numbers.

"Uplighting" trees, walls, and other landscape elements with spotlights or well lights creates magical nighttime features.

Basements and Garages

If you put the basement and garage at the bottom your home fix-up list, you can expect to feel a mix of emotions when it's finally time to tackle them. On the one hand, you'll be relieved that the tough stuff is behind you. No more painstaking finish work, no more deliberating over paint colors, no more experimenting with cleaning solutions for old pet stains. As unfinished spaces, garages and basements generally call for uncomplicated fixes, so now you can really begin to see the light at the end of the tunnel. On the other hand, that bright light of hope may be depressingly obscured by the mountains of junk you've been diverting to the garage and basement throughout the process of cleaning up the rest of the house.

If this scenario sounds familiar, the next step should be painfully clear: It's time for some serious de-cluttering. Not organizing. Not tidying up. But ruthless and decisive pitching of absolutely everything you don't need. This alone is the most effective thing you can do to make a basement or garage appealing to homebuyers (as well as spouses, renters, or in-laws). More than anything, basements and garages offer the promise and irresistible allure of empty space—for storage, hobbies, house projects, band practice, and much more. Everybody wants more space.

When the last heap of trash has been hauled away, the next step (after marveling at how much more room you have) need be nothing more than cleaning up the walls and floor and, in the garage, making sure the door and opener are running smoothly. Here, you'll find quick-fix projects for all of these areas, plus tips for dealing with basement moisture and a couple of garage upgrades that might make you wish you had spent a little less on your kitchen.

Basements

Home buyers are usually looking for one thing in an unfinished basement: clean, dry, empty space. There's no need for sellers to spend money on homey touches, like flooring or an acoustic-tile ceiling, in an effort to make this utility space seem more livable. Remember, a basement doesn't count toward a home's square footage, and even a finished basement won't necessarily raise your appraised value. If you want to improve the feel of your basement, add a few overhead light fixtures to brighten those creepy corners. Aside from that, a solid-looking concrete box is good enough.

Keeping Your Basement Dry

The last thing you want to see in a basement is water. Not only is moisture bad for stored items, it also promotes wood rot. Ongoing moisture can lead to mold growth, which in turn can

Testing basement walls for level and searching for signs of moisture are two of the many checks potential buyers will perform. But the most important thing you can do as a homeowner is make sure your basement is empty, dry, and well lit for showings.

ruin your indoor air quality. Understandably, house hunters are very wary of wet basements. Dampness can come from a range of sources, including condensation from appliances and AC systems, precipitation outdoors, and excess water in the ground. But the vast majority of basement moisture problems are due to improper drainage outside the house, usually caused by poor gutter drainage and/or improper grading around the house.

If moisture shows up in your basement after a heavy rain or snowfall, make sure your gutters are doing their job. Add extension pipes or flexible tubing to the ends of downspouts to carry roof runoff well away from the foundation. The ground around the house should slope down a minimum of one inch per foot for at least the first 10 feet from the foundation, to help keep surface water from pooling. If necessary, re-grade problem areas to promote natural drainage.

You can test for condensation by taping a two-foot-long strip of aluminum foil to the basement wall, sealing all edges of the foil with duct tape. After two days, peel off the foil. If it's damp on the exposed side, there's too much moisture in the interior air of the basement. If it's damp on the wall side, moisture is seeping in through the wall from the outside. Reduce air moisture by insulating all cold-water pipes in the basement, as well as any exposed air ducts if you have central air conditioning. Their cold surfaces promote condensation in humid weather. If your clothes dryer is in the basement, make sure it is properly vented to the outdoors. Excess humidity in rooms above can get into the basement, too, so make sure your bathrooms have good vent fans (and don't forget to use them!). Running a dehumidifier in the basement during damp or humid weather also helps reduce air moisture.

Basements with serious water problems, like frequent flooding or water coming up through the floor, require professional attention. However, don't do anything until you've corrected any gutter and drainage problems around the foundation.

Radon Testing

If you're preparing your house to go on the market, it's a good time to head off any unpleasant surprises that could get in the way of closing the deal. In basements, this means radon. A basic radon test kit will run about $30, including the lab processing fee. The test is easy to perform—just follow the simple steps on the kit and use the enclosed mail-in form. The results will let you know if you have a problem that could potentially hold up or even stop a sale in its tracks.

Gutter downspouts without extensions dump huge amounts of water right near the foundation, while an improper grade keeps surface water against the house. Downspout extensions and corrections to the grade solve many basement moisture problems.

What's That White Stuff on the Walls?

The chalky, white residue commonly found on basement walls is called efflorescence, and it's really nothing to worry about. Efflorescence is caused by water-soluble salts being carried to the surface by water leeching through the concrete or block masonry. This is a natural process, and all materials containing Portland cement can effloresce, including poured concrete, concrete block, and brick mortar. While the white stuff itself is harmless, it often indicates dampness or excess moisture on the other side of the wall. Because of this, efflorescence can help you locate drainage problems around your foundation.

Efflorescence does create a problem for waterproofing a basement wall, because the coatings won't stick to it. You have to remove the white stuff before applying the coating: Try a commercial masonry etching solution (most contain acid, such as sulfamic or muriatic acid), following the manufacturer's directions. If you're leaving the walls bare, you can simply brush off the bulk of the efflorescence residue so it's less visible. Washing it off with water alone won't make it disappear for long, since the water just activates more salts on the surface.

Remove efflorescence prior to coating a concrete or block basement wall. Make sure the cleaner is compatible with the wall coating; it's best if both come from the same manufacturer.

Repairing Basement Walls

Basement wall cracks less than ⅛ inch wide are normal and fairly common. Concrete block walls often develop cracks along mortar joints, due to settling, or pressure from water in the soil behind the wall (called hydrostatic pressure). *Note: If your basement walls have large or widespread cracking, or if a wall bows in more than one inch, have the foundation checked out by a professional.*

Though minor cracks that aren't growing seldom indicate structural problems, a crack that goes all the way through a wall creates an easy path for water seepage and insects. You can test the depth of a crack by inserting a wire and comparing the depth to the overall thickness of the wall. It's a good idea to seal all minor cracks with a high quality epoxy crack filler. Filling cracks is also necessary if you're planning to coat the wall with concrete paint.

Small holes and cracks can also be filled with hydraulic cement. Sold in dry powder form to be mixed with water, hydraulic cement sets up in about 10 to 15 minutes and quickly expands as it dries to form a tight plug in the cavity. This makes it capable of stopping a leak even as water is flowing in. To seal a cavity with hydraulic cement, clean out all loose material with a cold chisel and hammer. For a crack, chisel out the sides at the base, so the crack is wider at the bottom than at the surface, thus creating a triangular key to help hold the cement. Clean the repair area with a wire brush and a shop vacuum.

Mix the cement to a peanut butter consistency, following the manufacturer's directions. Dampen the crack with water, then fill the cavity with cement, smoothing it flush to the surface with a trowel. Work quickly; the cement begins to set up almost as soon as you mix it. To fill holes and gaps where the floor meets a wall, mix a thin batch of cement and pour it into the cavity until it's flush with the surface.

Tip: Shopping Smart

You'll be surprised at how little epoxy or hydraulic cement you'll need to plug even a good-sized crack. Buy the smallest container of either—look to spend about $5.

Seal minor cracks in concrete or block basement walls with epoxy crack filler. Smooth it flush with a wet finger to ensure a good seal and create a flat surface for wall coatings.

Painting Basement Walls

If your basement walls suffer from occasional dampness, a good coating of basement wall paint or surface cement can help. For best results, follow the manufacturer's directions carefully, and be sure to take care of any drainage problems (see page 134) beforehand to help keep water away from the basement walls. Do not expect that a simple coat of paint (even if it is called waterproofing paint) will rectify any water problems you may have in your basement. Apply these products purely for cosmetic purposes.

Basement wall paint goes on with a brush and roller, just like regular paint. It comes in a few basic colors, such as white, beige, gray, and blue, and in both oil-base and water-base formulas. Some products can be tinted with approved colorants. As with any paint, waterproofer can't hide surface flaws, but it does provide consistent coloring and a freshly renewed look. Its easy application makes for a good quick fix on most basement walls.

To coat your walls with this paint, complete all prep work recommended by the paint's manufacturer. Filling cracks and holes in the surface and removing efflorescence are typical prep projects. Scrub the surface thoroughly with a wire brush to remove all loose concrete or mortar and dirt. Wipe down the wall to remove dust. *Note: Waterproofer works best over bare masonry. If the wall has been painted, check with the manufacturer for recommendations.*

Apply the first coat with a stiff paintbrush, working the paint into all of the pores and fine cracks in the masonry surface. The coverage rate is important: You don't spread it out thinly like you do with regular paint. The manufacturer will specify how much to use in a given area so the coating is thick enough. Let the first coat dry as directed. Apply the second coat with a brush or a heavy-nap roller, being careful to cover any missed spots or pinholes left in the first coat. Let the second coat dry.

Hydraulic cement expands as it dries, creating a watertight seal. Repairs can be left as-is or be covered with masonry paint or waterproofer.

Garages

A well-maintained and spacious (or at least uncluttered) garage is an unqualified bonus for any home. Some house hunters inspect garages with little more than a cursory glance at the floor space, to see whether their cars would fit. Others do a thorough critical walkthrough, like a seasoned cook evaluating the layout and equipment of a kitchen. And some are simply swept away by the prospect of off-street parking. All will look for an automatic door opener.

It's up to you to decide what you or potential buyers want from a garage and to plan your fix-ups accordingly. As a bare minimum, a garage makeover should include cleaning all surfaces and inspecting the appearance of the walls and ceiling. If the walls are drywalled, patch any holes and repair failed seams following the steps on pages 60 to 61. You might go so far as to slap on a new coat of paint for a quick renewal. If the walls aren't covered, it's probably not worth the time and expense for sellers to finish them with new drywall. Instead, make sure the insulation (if there is any) is in good shape.

Check the operation of all doors and windows and make repairs accordingly. Give the windows a good cleaning—natural light adds an especially nice touch in a garage. With the walls and ceiling in decent shape, you can turn your attention to the floor.

For some reason, garage floors tend to get noticed almost as much as those in living spaces. And while no one expects perfection in a hard-used concrete slab, deep layers of oil stains and badly pitted concrete are unsightly and even a little off-putting. Remove old oil stains from a garage floor with a commercial concrete cleaner/degreaser. If the concrete is pretty beat up, you can repair cracks and fill holes following the techniques shown on pages 118 to 120. If you really want your garage floor to look snazzy, you can add a surface treatment, such concrete resurfacer (see pages 119 to 120) or epoxy coating. Both treatments do a great job of covering repair patches and old, discolored concrete for a totally renewed look.

Water damage is common when wallboard is installed too close to a garage floor. Replace damaged areas like this with strips of new drywall, keeping it at least 1" above the floor.

Flooring Finesse

If your garage floor is in unsightly disrepair and you don't have the time or inclination to repair and resurface for sale, consider the quick solution of rubber roll flooring. For around $1 per square foot, you can lay down an attractive, durable floor in a couple of hours.

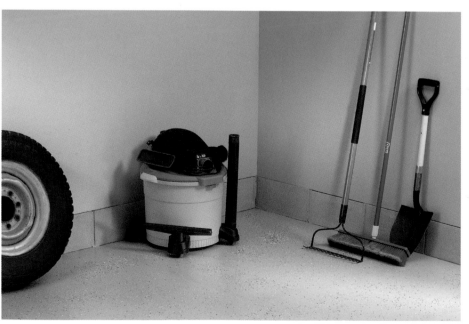

Epoxy-based garage floor paint costs about $50 a gallon, but you should be able to cover a single stall garage floor with one gallon. Once applied it is attractive, attention-grabbing, and easy to clean.

Tuning Up a Garage Door

Smart house hunters will open a garage door to check its operation. If you're a new owner, tuning up your garage door now can save you major headaches down the road. Begin your tune-up by tightening every mounting bolt you can find—on the hinge plates, lock assembly, track mounts and connector plates, and lift bars and handles. Replace any missing bolts. Next, check the alignment of the roller tracks that carry and guide the door. Ideally, the vertical sections of the tracks are installed plumb (perfectly vertical), from side to side and front to back.

Adjust the position of the door in relation to the frame by loosening the bolts securing the track to its mounting brackets on the wall. Move the tracks toward or away from the frame as needed, then tighten the bolts. When door tracks are out of plumb from side to side, the rollers can bind or, conversely, they can pull too far out of their hinge sleeves, resulting in rough travel and causing undo wear on the rollers. Adjust the side-to-side alignment by loosening the bolts where the track mounts meet the wall, then nudge the track sideways as needed (a rubber mallet helps with this) and retighten the bolts. Replace the light bulb if necessary.

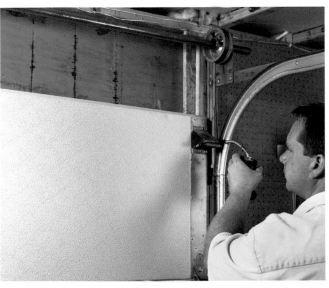

Begin the tune-up by lubricating the door tracks, pulleys, and rollers. Use a lightweight oil, not grease, for this job. The grease catches too much dust and dirt.

If the chain on your garage door opener is sagging more than ½" below the bottom rail, it can make a lot of noise and cause drive sprocket wear. Tighten the chain according to the directions in the owner's manual.

Lubricate the garage door opener drive chain or screw.

Test shutoff sensors to make sure they are operating correctly.

Resources and Photo Credits

Resources

Abatron Inc.
Wood restoration and repair products
As shown on page 112
www.abatron.com
800-445-1754

Andersen Windows
As shown on page 90
www.andersenwindows.com

Bath Wizard
Tub and sink repair kits
www.bathwizard.com
800-498-7093

Blaine Window Hardware, Inc.
www.blainewindow.com

FastenMaster
www.fastenmaster.com

Gel Gloss
Fiberglass and acrylic polishing compound
As shown on page 43
www.gel-gloss.com
800-243-3272

Kampel Enterprises, Inc.
SeamFil laminate repair compound
As shown on page 19
www.kampelent.com
800-837-4971

Repair-It-All
Vinyl and leather repair kits
As shown on page 19
www.repair-it-all.com
440-774-3900

Replacement Hardware Mfg., Inc.
www.replacementhardware.com

Safety Footwear shown in many
photos was provided courtesy of
Red Wing Shoe Company
www.redwingshoes.com

Welco Manufacturing Company
As shown on page 59
www.wel-cote.com

Photo Credits

Page 6: Eric Roth/www.Built-well.com
Page 7: istockphoto
Page 13: Eric Roth (for Tony Catalano/www.catalanoinc.com)
Page 28 (right, all): istockphoto
Page 33: © Arcaid/Alamy
Page 34 (top): Photo courtesy Moen
Page 55: istockphoto
Page 101: istockphoto
Page 108: Photo courtesy Armstrong Flooring
Page 116 (bottom): istockphoto
Page 124: istockphoto
Page 125 (left): © Per Karlsson-BKWine.com/Alamy
Page 128 (left): istockphoto
Page 128 (bottom right): Black & Decker
Page 130 (bottom): David Goldberg
Page 131 (left): istockphoto
Page 131 (right): Clive Nichols

Conversions

Metric Equivalent

	1/64	1/32	1/25	1/16	1/8	1/4	3/8	2/5	1/2	5/8	3/4	7/8	1	2	3	4	5	6	7	8	9	10	11	12	36	39.4
Inches (in.)	1/64	1/32	1/25	1/16	1/8	1/4	3/8	2/5	1/2	5/8	3/4	7/8	1	2	3	4	5	6	7	8	9	10	11	12	36	39.4
Feet (ft.)																								1	3	3 1/12
Yards (yd.)																									1	1 1/12
Millimeters (mm)	0.40	0.79	1	1.59	3.18	6.35	9.53	10	12.7	15.9	19.1	22.2	25.4	50.8	76.2	101.6	127	152	178	203	229	254	279	305	914	1,000
Centimeters (cm)							0.95	1	1.27	1.59	1.91	2.22	2.54	5.08	7.62	10.16	12.7	15.2	17.8	20.3	22.9	25.4	27.9	30.5	91.4	100
Meters (m)																								.30	.91	1.00

Converting Measurements

TO CONVERT:	TO:	MULTIPLY BY:		TO CONVERT:	TO:	MULTIPLY BY:
Inches	Millimeters	25.4		Millimeters	Inches	0.039
Inches	Centimeters	2.54		Centimeters	Inches	0.394
Feet	Meters	0.305		Meters	Feet	3.28
Yards	Meters	0.914		Meters	Yards	1.09
Miles	Kilometers	1.609		Kilometers	Miles	0.621
Square inches	Square centimeters	6.45		Square centimeters	Square inches	0.155
Square feet	Square meters	0.093		Square meters	Square feet	10.8
Square yards	Square meters	0.836		Square meters	Square yards	1.2
Cubic inches	Cubic centimeters	16.4		Cubic centimeters	Cubic inches	0.061
Cubic feet	Cubic meters	0.0283		Cubic meters	Cubic feet	35.3
Cubic yards	Cubic meters	0.765		Cubic meters	Cubic yards	1.31
Pints (U.S.)	Liters	0.473 (Imp. 0.568)		Liters	Pints (U.S.)	2.114 (Imp. 1.76)
Quarts (U.S.)	Liters	0.946 (Imp. 1.136)		Liters	Quarts (U.S.)	1.057 (Imp. 0.88)
Gallons (U.S.)	Liters	3.785 (Imp. 4.546)		Liters	Gallons (U.S.)	0.264 (Imp. 0.22)
Ounces	Grams	28.4		Grams	Ounces	0.035
Pounds	Kilograms	0.454		Kilograms	Pounds	2.2
Tons	Metric tons	0.907		Metric tons	Tons	1.1

Converting Temperatures

Convert degrees Fahrenheit (F) to degrees Celsius (C) by following this simple formula: Subtract 32 from the Fahrenheit temperature reading. Then mulitply that number by 5/9. For example, 77°F - 32 = 45. 45 × 5/9 = 25°C.

To convert degrees Celsius to degrees Fahrenheit, multiply the Celsius temperature reading by 9/5, then add 32. For example, 25°C × 9/5 = 45. 45 + 32 = 77°F.

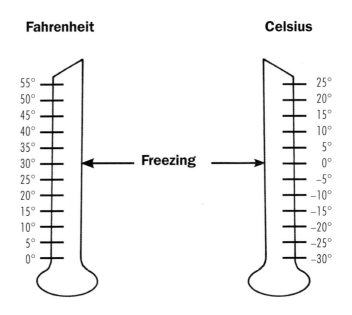

Fahrenheit   **Celsius**

← **Freezing** →

Index